Where Once We Feared Enemies

Inclusive Membership, Prophetic Vision, And The American Church

Nibs Stroupe

Edited By Chris Boesel

CSS Publishing Company, Inc., Lima, Ohio

WHERE ONCE WE FEARED ENEMIES

Some scripture quotations are from the New Revised Standard Version of the Bible, copy-
right 1989 by the Division of Christian Education of the National Council of the Churches
of Christ in the USA. Used by permission.

Library of Congress Cataloging-in-Publication Data

Stroupe, Nibs.
  Where once we feared enemies : inclusive membership, prophetic vision, and the American church / Nils Stroupe; edited by Chris Boesel.
    p. cm.
  ISBN 0-7880-2351-9 (perfect bound : alk. paper)
1. Presbyterian Church—Sermons. 2. Sermons, American. I. Boesel, Chris. II. Title.

BX9178.S88W44 205
252'.051—dc22

2005001238

For more information about CSS Publishing Company resources, visit our website at
www.csspub.com or e-mail us at custserv@csspub.com or call (800) 241-4056.

Cover design by Chris Patton
ISBN 0-7880-2351-9   PRINTED IN U.S.A.

This book is dedicated to
my mother,
Mary Stroupe,
who taught me about the love of God,
and
to my children,
David and Susan,
who continue to teach me
about the grace of God

Table Of Contents

Editor's Foreword

Oakhurst Presbyterian Church is unremarkable on the outside, but the congregation inside is quite remarkable ... middle class professionals, blue collar and pink collar workers, welfare recipients, old, young, and very young, black, white, Asian, gay and straight. All seem to feel comfortable there, and speak their minds.

Ted Clark, National Public Radio
"All Things Considered," April 10, 1994

At Oakhurst Presbyterian Church, there's a black Jesus in front, a white Jesus in back and folks of both colors in between ... Oakhurst ... is what diversity is all about: people of different races coming together not in the mournful, candle-bearing aftermath of some urban riot or the artificially arranged precursor to some political photo op, but because they want to be together.

Christopher John Farley, *Time* magazine
April 24, 1995

Race, America, Church: Sermons For Our Time And Place

Between 1994 and 1997 the "remarkable" congregation of Oakhurst Presbyterian Church was featured in stories by CBS Radio, CNN, NBC News, the *Wall Street Journal, The Christian Science Monitor, Time*, and NPR. In 1993, the church was included as a subject of a study conducted by Emory University which resulted in a book on cultural diversity in American churches titled *We Are The Church Together* (Trinity Press, 1996), co-authored by Charles R. Foster and Theodore Brelsford. In addition, *While We Run This Race* (Orbis, 1995), a book co-authored by the pastor and a lay member of the congregation chronicling the story of Oakhurst and its struggle with race, received the 1996 Book Award for the outstanding book on human rights from the Gustavus Myers Center for the Study of Human Rights. More recently, the church itself, along with Bishop Desmond Tutu, was honored by the Rollins School of Public Health and the Goizueta Business School with the 1999 Community Ministry Award in honor of Martin Luther King, Jr., Day.

As this brief resume suggests, in the mid-1990s Oakhurst Presbyterian Church found itself in the national spotlight — especially given the paradoxical aftermath of heightened tension and awareness with regard to issues of race following the troubling events involving Rodney King and O. J. Simpson. In the 1960s the sermons of Martin Luther King, Jr., roused both nation and church with a call to justice and racial equality. He provided a vision of a possible future, a glimpse of what justice might look like "on the red hills of Georgia": blacks and whites sitting down together in equality to break bread and share their lives. Thirty years on, however, what had become of the vision? In many sectors of the nation it seemed to have fallen upon hard soil, having been plucked away by birds of prey, scorched and withered over time, or choked out by thorns of entrenched resistance. The events surrounding Rodney King and O. J. Simpson had thrown this grim reality into glaring, painful relief. In a rare moment of collective soul-searching the nation refocused its vision and energies upon the role of race in America, opening the possibility of what appeared to be a genuine confrontation with its failure to follow through on the promise of the Civil Rights Movement — indeed, on the promise of its foundational creed: that all persons are created equal. In the midst of this dark night, the national media stumbled upon a surprising anomaly — a balm to sooth the nation's sin-sick soul. In the life of a small neighborhood church in Decatur, Georgia, the vision of Martin Luther King, Jr., appeared to have taken root and blossomed into a meager, yet stubborn, reality.

Reporters came. Stories were written. Hearts were moved and inspired. A wave of first-time visitors came to Oakhurst Presbyterian Church, fired with a new commitment to confront issues of race in their lives, in the church, and in the nation. But time trudged along its relentless journey. The prescribed time for serious national introspection and conviction was solemnly observed. Other compelling events — on both the national and international stage, both in Washington, D.C. and in Hollywood — pressed for the nation's attention. The nation, relieved, dutifully obliged. Weekly attendance at Oakhurst tapered off to its previous level of slow, incremental growth. The national ground hardened, the birds of prey plucked, the thorns choked. And still, from the pulpit of Oakhurst Presbyterian Church, week after week, sermons animated by a uniquely American theological vision continued to provide the sustenance vital for the difficult journey of incarnating Dr. King's dream into a living, day to day reality.

The attention and interest of the nation and the greater American church came and went, carried along by the rhythms, cycles, and necessities of the news media and the public appetite. This is no doubt to be expected with regard to the grave demands of justice and of the gospel. But the nation — and the church — are for all that no less in need of hearing both. And this, in the briefest compass, is the reason behind this book of sermons. There is a jewel of great price here, for the American church and for the nation at large. Its value is rooted in — but also extends beyond — the confrontation with racism and the promise of justice that constitute a central theme of these sermons and of the congregation to which they are addressed. These sermons are of vital importance because of their prophetic confrontation with a whole spectrum of idols that define the culture of the west, because of their radical vision of the identity and mission of the American church, and because of the hermeneutical and theological assumptions and commitments that fund this prophetic confrontation and vision.

The preacher of these sermons is a child of the church in the white South of the 1950s. While growing up in Helena, Arkansas, it was from this church that Gibson "Nibs" Stroupe received the great gift of a deep sense of the grace and love of God. That very same church taught Stroupe to believe that white people were superior to all others, especially black people. It taught him that men were superior to women, that money would buy him happiness, that guns would keep him safe, that gay and lesbian people were beyond the pale — all cultural beliefs that managed to intertwine themselves with the belief in God's saving grace. Stroupe's own journey, as well as the central thrust of his preaching and pastoral ministry, can be defined as a continuing struggle to loosen the hold of these idolatrous beliefs on his own heart and on the heart and life of the church, while preserving, strengthening, and proclaiming the faith and hope that is grounded in the grace and love of God known in Jesus Christ.

The social context of the Civil Rights Movement had a profound effect on Stroupe's development, raising challenging questions about his inherited assumptions regarding white supremacy. These questions led to a decisive turning point when, during the summer between his sophomore and junior years in college, Stroupe worked in a summer program in a church in New York City. During those months, Stroupe began to discover in earnest — in both exciting and disturbing ways — the humanity of black folks. And this surprising discovery entailed another — the discovery of his *own* humanity, a humanity no longer bound so tightly to race or gender or class, but rather to the dignity that he, together with the African-Americans he had come to know, received as a child of God. The realization of this profound and simple truth, that we belong to God and to one another — a truth he now understands to be as vital to our lives as it is extremely difficult to accept and to live — determined the fundamental direction and tone of Stroupe's life and eventual ministry from that summer in Brooklyn to the present.

Radicalized by this new sense of shared humanity in the grace and love of God, Stroupe went on to a vocation of both ministry and activism. He was a conscientious objector to the Vietnam War from 1970 to 1972. As his alternative service to the country, Stroupe helped found a halfway house in Nashville, Tennessee, for men getting out of prison. Graduating at the top of his class from Columbia Theological Seminary in 1975, Stroupe was ordained and served a small church in a low-income housing project as co-pastor, with his wife, Caroline Leach. Stroupe returned to prison ministry in Nashville in 1981, working with prisoners on death row and lobbying for prison reform in the state legislature. Stroupe and Leach came to Oakhurst Presbyterian Church in 1983, again as co-pastors.

Oakhurst, in the meantime, had been undergoing its own journey of struggle and conversion. In the mid-1960s the church was thriving in what was then an all-white neighborhood. At one time during this period it boasted a membership of over 850. At about that time a program of "urban renewal" began in downtown Atlanta. It included the construction of two major sports arenas and a civic center. Thousands of African-American families were driven out of those downtown areas and many moved east to Decatur, where the Oakhurst neighborhood is located. Their arrival touched off a steady stream of "white flight" from these residential areas, and between 1970 and 1990 the population of the Oakhurst neighborhood went from almost 100 percent white to 95 percent black. Not surprisingly, between 1963 and 1982 the membership of Oakhurst Presbyterian Church dropped from 850 to eighty. The vast majority of its members simply could not tolerate living and worshiping in the presence of black people.

This was, however, a period of strong pastoral leadership at Oakhurst. A succession of pastors attempted to open the church to the African-American families moving into the neighborhood. Despite the frustration of encountering consistent resistance from both the Session and the white membership of the church, these pastors did manage to open the door to a new possibility of being the church in this time and place. In 1970, Oakhurst received its first black member, Nate Mosby, who began a tradition of strong, black lay-leadership in the church. A small number of whites stayed. A growing number of African-Americans joined. But even as the small, struggling congregation was becoming truly integrated in terms of membership, significant barriers continued to divide the community. In 1982, there was still strong resistance to introducing elements of black church into the worship at Oakhurst, and to power-sharing in general across the racial divide. It was into this struggling, yet promising, context that Stroupe and Leach arrived in 1983.[1]

Church Identity: Who Is The Church? Whose Church Is It?

The story of race in America, while being foundational to both Stroupe's personal journey and the corporate journey of Oakhurst

Presbyterian Church, is not, however, the whole story. The scope of Stroupe's prophetic challenge has steadily broadened to include other difficult issues central to the American — and the human — condition. This growing breadth of vision arises from the crucible of conversion that has marked Stroupe's own journey of faith as it has continued to unfold at Oakhurst; conversions from white supremacy, from homophobia, from the worship of America and of materialism. This history — a history he understands to be ongoing, fully expecting to face more calls to conversion — has radically shaped Stroupe's understanding of what, and who, constitutes the life and identity of the church. What is the church called to *be*, and *who* is called to be the church? Pervading Stroupe's sermons with stubborn consistency is the conviction that the American church is a community for whom the idols and barriers of the world — skin color, money, consumer products, gender, sexual orientation, militarism — through which we seek identity and security, and by which we separate ourselves from our neighbor, have been brought down in Jesus Christ. The result is a vision of radically inclusive and egalitarian membership which has shaped and fed Oakhurst Presbyterian Church for over fifteen years, throwing open, and holding open its doors to all who would come.

Stroupe is aware, however, that it is not enough to simply create an integrated and diverse congregation in terms of numbers and percentages. For the church to truly answer its call and fulfill its mission as the church of Jesus Christ, power must be shared across lines of race, class, gender, and sexual orientation. Stroupe has discovered this to be the hardest lesson for the white folk at Oakhurst to learn, and live, in the church's struggle with race. It is also perhaps the most perennial issue, not easily overcome. And it is not confined to the issue of race. It can, and does, affect and shape the fundamental struggles in every dimension of church life.

For Stroupe, the resistance to sharing power in the church is ultimately a theological issue. It is a fundamental expression of our lack of faith and our penchant for idolatry. We do not share power because we do not believe in the promise of God to be present to the community in and through God's Spirit. Consequently, we allocate to ourselves the responsibility, and the power, to make the

Spirit present, to mediate the presence and work of the Spirit in the life, work, and worship of the church. The fear that the presence and the work of the Spirit will be effectively blocked if it is left in the hands of others is grounded in the belief that it is ultimately the work of *our own* hands, and *not* the free willing and moving of the Spirit, that mediates that presence and work. Whose church is it? For Stroupe, our unwillingness to share power is an expression of our incessant efforts to seize ownership of the church from its proper head, foundation, and source, the Spirit of God in Jesus Christ, and place it in our own hands.

It should be discernible at this point that Stroupe's radically inclusive vision of church identity is *not* an essentially political, social, or cultural vision, of interest primarily for political and/or sociological reasons. While political and social dimensions are most likely the reason why Oakhurst became of keen interest, for a time, to the reporters from NPR and *Time* magazine (cited above), and perhaps for the listening and reading public at large, they are not so for Stroupe. He understands the church as first and foremost a communal *theological* adventure, a community of praise and worship, as well as of mission and action. For Stroupe, it is not, properly speaking, a vision of radical inclusivity that lies at the center of church identity. That vision is a *consequence* of the fact that it is *God* who is at the center of the church's identity, life, and mission. Stroupe's thematic focus on the call to a radical inclusivity of church membership, and the complex diversity of the congregation to which such a call inevitably gives rise, is a consequence of a logically and thematically prior focus upon the one who is pleased that it should be so. A focus upon the one who not only calls us to incarnate such an odd and unlikely thing in world, but who is also its very ground of possibility. We should be careful not to conclude, however, that Stroupe's theological vision is theological *instead* of political and social. Rather, I suggest that Stroupe simply rejects the modern differentiation of the theological and political spheres. His vision is *both* political and theological, all the way down.[2]

Stroupe reminds us of who we are, as church and as human beings, by reminding us of who *God* is, of the one to whom we belong, of the one who is at the center of our lives, and of history and of creation. The explicitness of Stroupe's social and political vision notwithstanding, the Oakhurst congregation hears a word preached about the God known in Jesus Christ that exceeds and cannot be reduced to moral, ethical, or socio-political categories. Neither is that word reducible to a passionate commitment to enact the church's prophetic mission and work in the world, though it is essentially related to that passion, commitment, work, and mission. Though an unapologetic political activist and social visionary, Stroupe is primarily, first and last, a pastor, preacher, and theologian of the Good News of the Christian gospel. His social and political vision of church membership, work, and mission is grounded in a *theological* vision. It is rooted in and springs from — *and is continually challenged and transformed by* — theological assumptions and biblical claims about the strange and unwieldy God that is known in the history, person, and work of Jesus Christ.

But there is a dialectical complexity that is fundamental to the uniqueness of Stroupe's theological and prophetic voice. For Stroupe, we cannot worship or serve — indeed, know — God *without* our neighbor in the pew (or on the street) who is different from ourselves. In the many situations in which members of Oakhurst join hands in prayer, Stroupe regularly reminds those gathered that it is in the hand we hold that God comes to us. It is in the hand we hold that we meet God. This is especially true when the one extending that hand is different from ourselves. One of the most central, recurring themes of both Stroupe's preaching and corporate prayer is the claim that we meet God when we hold the hands of those who we thought were our enemies, and who we discover to be the sisters and brothers for whom our heart longs. For Stroupe, our encounter with God in Christ — in both the church and the world — is incarnated in and through the neighbor and the stranger, and most especially, in and through the least of these, the poor, the oppressed, and the needy.

Given that Stroupe is convinced that we meet and come to know God in and through the neighbor and the stranger, it would now seem that the human encounter is weighted with a certain priority over the divine encounter. But for Stroupe, the neighbor and the stranger are always already theologically determined. We meet and come to know God in and through the neighbor and the stranger — the poor and the needy — as they are encountered as *children of God*, as the poor are encountered and received as *God's* poor. And so goes the dialectical movement between our encounter with and knowledge of God and our encounter with and knowledge of the neighbor. This movement would seem to make it impossible to fix an absolute chronological or epistemological priority to either encounter. However, for Stroupe, there is nevertheless a *theological* priority, or ordering, within which this dialectic has its movement: the theological assumption and claim that God is the center of our lives and of all life. While it is true, then, that for Stroupe we meet God in our encounter with the stories of the neighbor and the stranger, these are always stories of those who are already addressed (whether acknowledged or not) by *another* story — the story of the God witnessed to in the Bible and known in the history, person, and work of Jesus Christ.

Finally, if Oakhurst Presbyterian Church has been praised as a rare and precious anomaly in the contemporary life of the American church, as well as of the nation at large, how much more so the sermons which have shaped the struggle, growth, and identity of this church? Not only does this collection of Stroupe's sermons give us access to the theological and biblical vision funding the life of this "remarkable" church, they give us a glimpse of this life itself. The value of these sermons is underwritten by the story of the local church to which, and in which, they are preached. These sermons attain their universal import not over and above their local particularity, but precisely by virtue of their local connection, audience, and concern.[3] It is as sermons for *an* American church that they achieve their significance as sermons for *the* American church.

Chris Boesel
Drew University
January 16, 2004

1. This history of Oakhurst Presbyterian Church is covered much more extensively in a new book co-authored by Stroupe and Caroline Leach, *O Lord, Hold Our Hands: How a Church Thrives in a Multicultural World* (Louisville, Kentucky: Westminster John Knox Press, 2003). See also the book co-authored by Stroupe and Inez Fleming, *While We Run This Race: Confronting the Power of Racism in a Southern Church* (Maryknoll, New York: Orbis Press, 1995).

2. I owe this insight and its careful articulation to fellow Oakhurst member, Ted Smith. I received and made liberal use of critical suggestions from both Smith and Susan Hylen, colleagues who gave generously of their time and energy to read an earlier draft of the manuscript.

3. It is for this reason that we have purposely *not* edited out Stroupe's illustrative references to particular events and sites within the neighborhood and the city, or to political events and personalities on both the local and national level, that might, on one reading, seem to restrict the universal relevance of his message. Again, we simply do not agree with the basic assumption of this reading. Our conviction is that sermons only find their proper universal significance to the extent that they address the cultural, geographical, and temporal particularity of their contexts. Therefore, we have chosen to include these culturally, geographically, and temporally particular references, and provide footnotes giving further information necessary for the reader to appreciate the particular context in which the sermon is being preached.

A Word From The Preacher

It is a humbling and exciting and scary experience for a preacher to see his sermons being printed for an audience larger than the original congregation to which the sermons were preached. I give thanks to Chris Boesel for his editing and for his thoughtful and provocative foreword and afterword — I learned a lot about myself there! I want to thank my partner in life and in ministry, Caroline Leach, for her continuing revelation to me of the startling grace of God. I want to thank the rest of my family and circle of friends who continue to love me and challenge me and to help me discern the grace and call of God. Most of all, I want to thank the congregation of Oakhurst Presbyterian Church, where all these sermons were preached. As Chris indicates in his introduction, the church is where I learned all of the language of the quest for God, and the church is where I continue to wrestle with it. Oakhurst has been an extraordinary place in my life, a place where I have been loved and challenged and deepened.

One final word from the preacher: please read the biblical passages that are the texts for these sermons. They are the ground for the sermons, and indeed the purpose of the sermons is to help us all engage God and our stories with the story mediated through the biblical witness.

Reverend Nibs Stroupe

Call To Worship

Twice a year, on Visitors' Sunday and on Oakhurst's anniversary, Stroupe takes the opportunity to retell a bit of the Oakhurst story in the context of a biblical passage. The following reflection upon Mary's encounter with the risen Jesus, and how that story continues to shape and give meaning to the story of Oakhurst, was given on just such an occasion. It is an opportunity for visitors and members alike to walk again the rich narrative ground from which the recurring themes of Stroupe's homiletic voice have grown and from which they continue to receive nourishment. These themes serve as the headings for the various groupings of sermons collected here. As the frontispiece of this collection, this sermon about Mary's, and Oakhurst's, encounter with the risen Jesus amidst the power of death offers the reader a glimpse of the local context in which all of these sermons are given and heard.

Walking Through The Graveyard
John 20:1-18
Visitors' Sunday, May 16, 1999

This is the last Sunday of Eastertide. Next Sunday is Pentecost, when we celebrate the birth of the church. Jesus didn't rise from the dead just so individuals could be saved but rather to build a community of believers who serve God and who serve the world. The church is called to be this community. We will celebrate that gift and call next Sunday Pentecost. Today we will finish out Eastertide with one more encounter with the Resurrection, the account of Mary Magdalene coming to the tomb but not being able to recognize the risen Jesus.

Mary Magdalene is important in the history of the church and in the life and ministry of Jesus. Luke's Gospel tells us that Jesus healed Mary of seven demons. In gratitude and response, Mary Magdalene follows Jesus from Galilee to Jerusalem and joins in a group of women who provide money for the ministry of Jesus. According to Luke, it's not the men who are putting up the money to support Jesus. It's the women. The church hasn't changed much in that regard. It's women who support the church.

Mary Magdalene is the only person mentioned in all four gospel accounts of the Resurrection. In the midst of all the conflicting details about what went on where and who saw what, Mary Magdalene's presence at the tomb is the only constant in all four of the gospels. There are a lot of books about Jesus that did not make it into the Bible, and Mary Magdalene figures prominently in some of these. In one she is a rival to Peter in leadership; it's not clear who is the most important. In another book, she is the central figure who replaces Jesus in the circle of disciples. In yet another, which was made popular in *Jesus Christ, Superstar*, she is the lover of Jesus. Whatever the interpretation, Mary Magdalene was clearly a powerful force in the life of Jesus and in the life of the early church.

Given this background, why in the world doesn't Mary recognize the risen Jesus when she sees him at the tomb? Why is it that she can't see who he is? She can't recognize him when she sees him, and she doesn't recognize him when she hears him. She thinks that he is the groundskeeper for the cemetery. Doesn't it seem unbelievable that she doesn't recognize him? It does to me. I believe that I would recognize the risen Jesus if he was standing before me. It is unbelievable that Mary Magdalene doesn't recognize him. What's going on?

This is what's going on: the power of death. The power of death prevents Mary Magdalene and the other disciples from recognizing the risen Jesus. It's the same power of death that prevents disciples in every age from recognizing the risen Jesus. The biblical witness wants to make it clear — to disciples in every generation — that the first disciples of Jesus, that first generation of women and men who followed Jesus, had a very difficult time recognizing the risen Jesus. The biblical witness emphasizes that it's not just Mary Magdalene who has a difficult time. Cleopas and another disciple walk with the risen Jesus for seven miles on the road to Emmaus, but they do not recognize him. Peter doesn't recognize him when Jesus is fixing breakfast for him. Thomas won't believe any of it until he puts his hands right into the wounds. Others also fail to recognize him. They simply do not believe that Jesus is risen from the dead.

The Bible is realistic about what it means to be a human being and about the power of death in our lives. Death shuts down our hearts, blunts our vision, and closes our ears to God's voice. Mary Magdalene doesn't recognize the risen Jesus because she is held in the grip of death. She sees no possibilities for life. After all, she is not going to the hospital to visit a sick Jesus, praying for him to live. She is going to a graveyard to anoint a dead body. As Mary comes to the graveyard, she knows how it works. Jesus is dead. The Jesus movement that had inspired her so much is over. Mary comes to the tomb of Jesus out of loyalty to him, to be sure, but it is his dead body that she is coming to anoint. She is not looking for a risen Lord.

When she sees that the stone has been rolled away from the tomb, she does not think, "Hallelujah! Jesus is risen from the dead!" She is unable to imagine that possibility. Rather, she thinks that someone has stolen the body. She goes to get some of the male disciples to help her find the body. She is held in the icy grip of death. Her senses, her imagination, her heart are all captured by death. Even when the risen Jesus stands in front of her, she does not recognize him, so strong is the grip of death.

This biblical story wants us to consider the power of death in our lives, also. Most of the time we don't recognize the risen Jesus in our midst. This story asks us to think about the deals that we make with death, about how we accept the world's definitions of ourselves and of all of life. This is how it works: If there are homeless people in the United States, it must be because they are lazy or drug addicts. That's why they are homeless. That's the world's definition of this situation, the definition that's rooted in death. If there are poor people in the United States, it's because they don't want to work. Those are the definitions of death. Why go and demonstrate against Grady Hospital's raising prescription prices for the poor?[1] You can't do anything about it. And, even if Grady gets more county funding, the county will simply take that money from another part of the budget that serves the poor. So, don't try to do anything. Just let death have its dominion. That's how death works in our lives. It asks us to dismiss the story of the risen Jesus in our midst. And, it often works. We do indeed fail to recognize the risen Jesus in our midst.

This story reminds us of our own encounter with the resurrection of Jesus. It's a nice story. It's wonderful to come to church and celebrate Easter. It's a comforting thought, and we hope that it says something about life after death. But, what does it have to do with the real world, the world in which we are living right now? What does it have to do with the bombs falling in Kosovo at this moment? What does the resurrection of Jesus have to do with the ethnic cleansing in Serbia? What does it have to do with teenagers killing their peers in Colorado and both Cobb County and Cherokee County in Georgia?[2] What does the resurrection of Jesus have to do with the fact that it seems rich people are always getting their

23

way in this country? What does the resurrection of Jesus have to do with the prescription prices being raised at Grady Hospital? What does it have to do with the budget cuts for human services in Fulton County? What does the resurrection have to do with men dominating women? What does it have to do with a pace of life so frenetic and so frantic that we can hardly catch our breath? What does the resurrection of Jesus have to do with that sense of emptiness and hunger that we sometimes allow ourselves to glimpse in our own lives? What does the resurrection have to do with these things in the world where we live?

The biblical witness tells us that the resurrection of Jesus has *everything* to do with this kind of world. Indeed, it is in this kind of world that Jesus was born, had his ministry, upset folk, was executed as a revolutionary, and was raised from the dead. It is in this kind of world, the world in which we live, the world that we know, that the risen Jesus now moves and lives. Not in a perfect world where everyone is nice and loving and wonderful, but in a world gripped by death. The biblical witness asks us to look for Jesus in a world where everything is not wonderful, in a world where we have trouble recognizing the risen Jesus: "if we could just see you, Jesus!" This story tells us that the risen Jesus often stands in front of us, but death is so powerful and pervasive that we cannot recognize him.

The biblical witness is nothing if it is not realistic about the world and about who we are. It presents a realistic view of the world and of the first disciples, and it notes the continuing power of death in their lives, and in ours. It seems grim on that level because it wants disciples in every age to take seriously a promise that it proclaims, a promise that is real and true in our world, this day, this moment. That promise is the other experience that Mary Magdalene had in that graveyard on that first Easter morning. Surrounded by death, gripped by death, she could not recognize the risen Jesus. And yet, she is given life. She's offered new life. The scales fall from her eyes and her heart, and she recognizes the risen Jesus.

When Jesus saw that she did not recognize him, he didn't scold her. "Mary, don't you know anything? Don't you remember what

I said? Don't you know who I am? Can't you be faithful for just one moment?" Rather, he calls her name, "Mary." Her eyes and her ears and her heart are opened! She sees and hears that the risen Jesus is loving her and calling her, not when she's got all the answers, not when she's perfect, but when she's struggling, when she's gripped by death and sees no possibilities. And then, Mary Magdalene does recognize him, and she comes alive! She touches that passion again, that passion that Jesus had awakened in her when he healed her. She runs to hug him, and she runs to tell the other disciples, "I have seen the Lord!" She shares the great news, but many of the other disciples don't believe it. Luke's Gospel tells us that the men dismiss the witness of the women — they are just hysterical women who can't deal with the realities of life and death. But the men, too, will come to believe.

The biblical witness wants us to understand that this kind of possibility is in the world *now*, that the risen Jesus is not just something that happened 2,000 years ago on Easter morning. The risen Jesus is in our midst now, loving us and calling us. Not when we're perfect, not when we get our lives together, but when we're struggling; when we, too, are gripped by death and don't see any possibilities for life. The biblical witness tells us that we have the opportunity to experience what Mary Magdalene experienced in that graveyard. To hear our names called, to hear that we are somebody, to hear that we matter in a crazy and impersonal world. To hear that we have the opportunity to come alive like Mary, to touch our passion and to hear that we are children of God. To hear that our primary definition is not our bank account or our Social Security number, not the size of our home, not our racial classification, not our gender, not our sexual orientation, not our nationality, not any of those categories that the power of death tries to tell us are ultimate. Rather our primary definition is what Mary Magdalene heard in that graveyard when Jesus called her name, "Mary," daughter of God, defined by the love of God that she knew in Jesus Christ. This is the same Jesus who calls our names as daughters and sons of God.

Walking through the graveyard, that's what Mary was doing, looking for death, expecting death. This church has known that journey through the graveyard, that struggle with the power of death. We used to be all of one kind. We had almost 900 white members in the early 1960s. Then black folk began to move into the neighborhood, and many white folk in this church discovered that they believed more in the power of race than they believed in the power of the gospel. Many of the white folk fled from this neighborhood, and this church. Over a twenty-year period, this church's membership dropped from 900 to eighty. It was a time of depression here, knowing the power of death. It was a time of looking at the death of Oakhurst Presbyterian Church.

Yet, some white folks stayed here because they heard their names called. They began to hear a new definition of themselves. They stayed and began to come alive, to come out of the tomb of racism where the power of death rules. They began to come alive, to hear that racial classification is not the final word. They began to live out of a new definition. And some black folks came here, recognizing the need to build a community of faith that welcomed all people, a community that began to rejoice in diversity rather than seeing it as a problem.

So here we are. We have survived. We are beginning to thrive. We've had to confront many categories of the world in our journey together. We thought that affirming diversity meant only welcoming people of different colors, but we've learned that it means welcoming women as equal partners with men. We've learned that it means trying to put people who are poor with people who are comfortable. We've learned that it means putting people with Ph.D.s with people who cannot read. We've learned that it means coming together with people whom we thought were strange and maybe even our enemies — straight folk with gay and lesbian folk. We've had many struggles here as we've sought to come alive, and we continue to have struggles. But, we *are* coming alive here. We are finding hope and possibility and courage here, that we can be witnesses in a crazy world. We're hearing our names called, and like Mary, we are beginning to recognize the risen Jesus in our midst.

We're not quite perfect here. (You don't have to laugh so loudly about that, and I don't need that many "Amen" choruses from you!)

We are not perfect here. We make many mistakes. We disappoint one another, and we hurt one another. We anger one another. And yet, we believe that this journey is what the biblical witness is about. Being able to hear those kinds of feelings and emotions, being able to challenge and confront one another, and being able to go to a deeper level with one another in order to grow in the faith. We are discovering that black folk and white folk can listen to one another, that we can cross the great racial divide that is so pervasive in our culture. We are discovering that we need one another here, in all our diversity; that we need gay and lesbian folk to tell us straight folk what life is like; that we need poor folk to tell us comfortable folk what life is like.

This is a difficult and, at times, disturbing journey. That's often the way that God works in our lives. It might have been that a white person came up and shook your hand this morning. Or, it may be that a black person came up and hugged you. It might be our emphasis that women are equal partners here. It might be that we emphasize that gay and lesbian folk are called to be leaders here. Or, it might be that you feel uncomfortable as folks lift up our vulnerabilities when we share concerns and joys for prayers. There are all kinds of places where we find some disturbing things here. We don't do them to be disturbing, but we know that the categories by which death grips us do not give up easily. We need to practice life together in all our diversity, and that practice is sometimes disturbing.

It is a struggle here, but it is also life-giving here. We find life here because we are enabled to go deeper into ourselves and touch that passion that calls out to God, to find our true definition as children of God. We are not finally defined by our bank account or gender or sexual orientation or racial classification. We are defined as daughters and sons of God. We find life here because we are empowered to reach out to others to discover not the enemies we feared but the brothers and sisters for whom our hearts long.

That is what brings me back here. That's what brings most of us back here — the power of gospel, the life-giving power of the risen Jesus. It is the power that enables us to come alive in a world where death tells us to give up and give in. It's the power that enables us to see God in places where no one believes that God can be. It enables us to reach out and touch those whom the world tells us are enemies and instead find friends. It is the power that enables us to come alive in the graveyards of our lives. It's the power that speaks to us and calls our names. It's the power that helps us to recognize our true calling. Our true calling is not to be consumers. It is not to be racists. It is not to be sexists. It is not to be dominators. It is to be brothers and sisters in a community of faith that upholds one another and that seeks justice. That is our true calling, and that is the power that fills us up and goes down into us and sends us out into the world, proclaiming as Mary did, "I have seen the Lord!" Amen? Amen.

---

1. In 1892, Grady Memorial Hospital was chartered to provide health care for the poor and the sick of Atlanta, Georgia. On March 15, 1999, Grady implemented a policy that would require even the most poor to pay for clinic visits and to pay a minimum of $10 co-payment for each of their prescriptions and medical supplies. In response to this move, the Grady Coalition arose to protest this action. Oakhurst Church was part of this Coalition.

2. This refers to teenagers killing other teenagers at Columbine High School in Colorado and in two counties in the north metropolitan Atlanta area.

Struggling With God

These sermons are taken from a series on 1 Samuel. Thematically, they pick up on the tone of disorientation experienced by Mary when, confronted by the risen Jesus, she is unable to recognize him. In these sermons on God's journey with Israel, especially through the leadership of Samuel, the people of God share Mary's disorientation in their encounters with God. They must continually rediscover that the living God who has called them into relationship is not identical with their expectations. Israel and Samuel are both continually disconcerted and surprised at how God chooses to move in fulfilling God's promises. For Stroupe, these biblical stories confront us as realistic accounts of the continued struggle of disorientation and surprise experienced by all God's people in their journey through history with the living God.

God In A Box
1 Samuel 4:5-22
June 28, 1998

How many of you have seen the movie, *Raiders Of The Lost Ark*? Raise your hands. All right, just about everybody. The ark that is in the movie is the ark that is being described in today's scripture passage. It is a central part of chapter 4 of 1 Samuel. It's really a big box, about the size of our communion table, and it is very important in Israel's history. Exodus 25 tells us that Moses made the Ark of the Covenant as a container for the Ten Commandments. Numbers and Joshua tell us that the Israelite people were led through the wilderness into the promised land, with the Ark of the Covenant going before them. Over the years, it came to be seen as the place where God lived. Where is God? Where can you be the closest to God? In the Ark of the Covenant, God comes to be identified with the Ark.

In our scripture passage for today, we see the battle with the Philistines being lost, and so the Israelites pull out all the stops. They bring the Ark of the Covenant into battle with the Philistines. The Philistines are a difficult enemy for Israel. They've appeared previously in the Hebrew Scriptures. Samson fought against them in the book of Judges. They will continue to plague Israel throughout the history of the Hebrew Scriptures. Indeed, David rises to power as king of Israel because he is able to contain the Philistines. Not even the great David, however, can conquer the Philistines.

This struggle between Israel and the Philistines has had a profound effect on the Western world. One of the dictionary definitions of a Philistine is a person who is a slug, a person who has no cultural or aesthetic value. They would be called a "Philistine." But even more important for the west — and indeed the entire world — the Romans used a word in Latin to describe the area where the Philistines lived. That Latin word is *Palestina*, and that Latin word has come to be used to describe the entire area west of the Jordan River, "Palestine." So, even to this day, the ancient history and the ancient enmity between Israel and the Philistines continues. The Israelites continue to be in deadly conflict with their ancient enemy, the Philistines, now called the Palestinians. This conflict affects all of us. Modern Israel has indicated "never again" — we will never yield our land again. We will never yield to the Philistines, to the Palestinians. And Israel has the bomb, and we know that they may take us to the brink and beyond before they yield their land again.

This is one of the legacies of today's scripture. Its roots are deep in ancient history and long-seated conflict and even today it bears bitter fruit. Our scripture for today is one of bitterness and despair and death. A few weeks ago, Caroline asked me what I was preaching on this Sunday so that she could prepare the packets for the children during worship. She read the passage, came back, and said, "Are you sure that you want to preach on *this* passage?" And, my answer was, "Yes, I do."

The prophecy given to Eli in chapter 2 of 1 Samuel by an unknown prophet, and the vision given to Eli through the young boy Samuel in chapter 3, these are now fulfilled in chapter 4, as was indicated in the scripture reading today. Both of Eli's sons are killed on the same day. The sons, Phineas and Hophni, who are supposed to carry on the priestly line of their father Eli, have instead led the people into idolatry. As we see in this fourth chapter, this idolatry leads to death for these sons, and for the people of Israel.

Now, that's bad enough, to lose both of your sons on the same day. But for Eli and for Israel, things are much worse. Not only are the sons killed, not only do the Philistines win the battle, but they capture God! They capture the Ark of the Covenant, where God lives. The mighty God that defeated Pharaoh, their God is now captured by the Philistines, and the Ark of the Covenant is taken into the Philistine camp. It is unimaginable for the Israelites. God is captured. It is terrible, debilitating, annihilating news. It is so disturbing that when Eli hears it, he falls over dead. It is so disheartening that when the pregnant wife of Phineas hears the news, she goes into labor, gives birth to a son, naming him Ichabod, meaning, "the glory has vanished," and then she dies. How would you like to be Ichabod and remember your birthday? To remember the death of your mother, the death of your father, your uncle, your grandfather, and worst of all, the capture of God! It is a story that ends in disaster for Israel. The priestly line is destroyed, the Ark where God lives is captured, and death and despair win the day.

This story speaks of a fundamental shift for Israel in its view of God. To us in the modern world, it may seem silly to talk about God living in a box. But we must remember how important the Ark of the Covenant has been for Israel. It contains the Law, which is at the center of their lives, and it has led them through the wilderness and into the promised land. God came to be identified with this box, and Israel came to identify itself with this box. When they start losing the battle to their ancient foe, the Philistines, they call God out to help them. They call God out to help them in the fight. Since this is God's land, and since this is God's home, surely God will fight for them against the Philistines. Surely God is on their side and will bring them victory.

There is great despair in Israel when the Ark is captured, for it means that God has failed. God has been captured. It is a terrible lesson for Israel. They will begin to learn, as we will learn, in the next chapters of 1 Samuel, that God is more than the Ark of the Covenant. God doesn't live in the box. God is not limited to the box where the Israelites thought God lived. God is not defeated by the capture of the Ark of the Covenant. Indeed, the Philistines, and the Israelites, come to learn that God still has power. Chapters 5 and 6 of 1 Samuel tell us intriguing stories about people who touch that Ark, about the plagues that came to the Philistine camp because the Ark of the Covenant is in their midst. The Philistines finally end up sending the Ark back to Israel. "You can have this thing," they say. "It is a curse on us!" They send great gifts to Israel to induce them to take back this box. God is moving in ways that Israel could not imagine, and though there is death and despair in Israel, God is moving. God has already called a new leader, Samuel, even before the Ark is captured. In chapter 7, we will see his leadership. Israel learns a difficult lesson about trying to box

God in, about trying to confine God, about trying to put God in a place where we know God belongs.

This story speaks to God's people in every age about the peril of trying to keep God in a box, of believing that we've got God figured out and boxed in. We all tend to try to identify God with our beliefs, with our approaches to life. We want to think that God likes the way we live. We try to get God to fit into the boxes in our lives. We try to keep God boxed up and sometimes up on the shelf. When we really need God, when things get rough in our lives, we want to bring God off the shelf to help us, hoping that God will bless our visions and our dreams, just as the Israelites hoped in their battle with the Philistines. We feel better because we bring the God-box out, and we know that God will bring victory to us. Today's story in 1 Samuel points to the dangers of that process, of seeking to keep God in a box, whether the box we use is the Ark of the Covenant, whether it's skin color, whether it's money or economic status or gender or sexual orientation or nationality or any of those other boxes that we use to seek to confine God. This story reminds us in a stark way that God is deeper and wider and broader than our categories. God is not male. God is not white. All of those kinds of categories that we like to use for God are shattered by this story. We are reminded that God doesn't fit into those boxes.

When we seek to put God in a box, as Israel sought to do, when we bring God off the shelf to defend our categories, we often find that our boxes and our categories are shattered and scattered. We often face the death and despair and destruction and loss of meaning that Israel faced when the Ark of the Covenant was captured. Eli fell over and died not because his sons were killed but because God had been captured.

What Israel learned, and what we are asked to learn, is that God is not confined to our boxes and our categories. God is much more than we can ever imagine. A lesson like this is often bad news for us. It was for Israel when they learned that the Ark of the Covenant did not confine God. It is a difficult revelation when we learn that our categories do not fully contain and confine God. That's hard to hear. I still think of God as a man. Everybody knows that God is male — Big Daddy in the sky. But I've had many revelations that remind me that God is not male. I also thought for a long time that God is white. I've had difficult revelations that remind me that God is not white. And I surely believed that God is middle class. Yet, I've had difficult revelations to remind me that God is not middle class. It is in these kinds of revelations that despair and the abyss of death often visit us. It is difficult, a humbling process. That's what Israel experienced in this story. It's often bad news when we find out that God is not in the box that we thought God was in.

Yet, this lesson is also good news. The good news that God will not be captured by our boxes. God will not be captured by the Philistines of this world. And, even more, there is the good news that God will not be confined by the Christians of this world. God doesn't ordain that white men should rule the world. God doesn't ordain that people who have money should rule the world. Those are our categories and our beliefs. To have these revelations is difficult, but it is also good news. It gives us the ability to go out into the world and struggle with the principalities and powers, following God who is already out there, not sitting in the boxes where we thought God was. It's good news that God is powerful beyond our categories, that God continues to move and to work, even when we are wallowing in despair and resentment.

There is some other good news in this revelation, the good news that God won't give up on us, even as we wallow in despair, even as we are mad at God for not staying in our boxes. God won't give up on us. The capture of the Ark of the Covenant does not end Israel's story. Indeed, that story is really just beginning. God already has plans for this loose confederacy of tribes, even as the Ark is captured. God has already called forth a new leader named Samuel. Samuel's waiting. So is David. So is Isaiah. So is Huldah. So is Mary, the mother of Jesus, and John the Baptist. And Jesus. And Martha and Peter and Priscilla and Paul and a whole host of witnesses throughout the generations. Witnesses who have responded to the God who has moved out of the boxes, into our hearts and into the world. God's work with the covenant people is just beginning in this story in 1 Samuel, a story that seems so full of despair and death. God is already moving into new places. The story of God and God's people will be reformed and reshaped again and again and again, and it continues this morning. It's being reshaped in our hearts today, in the hearing and the sharing of this story.

That reformation is bad news on one level, because we brought a lot of categories into worship this morning, categories that we'd like to use to confine God. But God is constantly moving beyond us, out of our boxes, deeper into our hearts and into the world. Yet, it is profoundly good news on another level. The God we see in this story, not captured by the Philistines, not confined by the Israelites or the Christians, is still moving in our lives. The God who emerges in this story is the rock of our salvation. This is an ancient and old and despairing story. The enmity between the Israelites and the Philistines continues at this very moment. And the God who moves in our midst and in their midst continues to shatter our categories and our boxes, calling us to find our true place and true identity. Who are we? We're God's people, able to struggle with the categories of the world, seeking to find God's truth and God's grace in our midst. We are asked to hear that God will shatter our categories if we begin to worship them and seek to confine God to them. But, we are also asked to hear the good news that God will not give up on us, that God will supply the grace and power for us to live outside the boxes and the categories. God will help us to live as God's people. We are the people of God. Let us follow God into all kinds of places that we thought we could never go, would never go. There we will find God already waiting for us. Amen.

Living Between God And Egypt
1 Samuel 8:1-22
July 12, 1998

This is an important chapter in the history of Israel. It notes the beginning of Israel as a nation, and it is filled with ambiguity and ambivalence. What's recorded here is not July fourth fireworks and not great thanksgiving for the memory of the beginning of the monarchy. What is recorded here is a sense of loss. Why do we have a king? Why are we living like this? This chapter seeks to answer those questions. It indicates both blessing and curse in this development.

Samuel, the great prophet and judge, has grown old, as we heard in this morning's scripture. In a touch of irony, Samuel's sons are like the sons of Samuel's predecessor, Eli. They are corrupt and self-seeking. The elders of the tribes of Israel rise up and ask for a king so that the corruption will end. The emphasis here is that justice is being perverted. We must note that the demand for a king arises not out of an external military threat but rather from an internal threat — the loss of justice, the collapse of the system which brings justice. As we learned from chapter 7 last week, God delivered the tribes of Israel from the Philistines not to establish a powerful nation that ruled the world, but rather to establish justice. And now, that justice is being perverted.

Samuel reacts with anger and sadness at the request of these elders. He is angry that after all he has done for these tribes of Israel, he, and his line, are being rejected by the people. They don't want his sons. He is sad because he knows why they don't want his sons. His sons have failed. Does Samuel now understand what his mentor Eli felt when Eli's sons perverted justice, and Samuel replaced them? Does Samuel now understand how difficult and complex it is to try to pass from one generation to the next the values and beliefs of the past?

Yet, even as Samuel feels dejected and rejected, he remembers who he is. He is a servant of God, and he takes his concern to

God, who is at the center of his life. Israel is not the center of Samuel's life, God is. Samuel prays to God about this request for a king from these elders, and he receives a stunning answer. "You shall answer their request in the affirmative. And, don't feel rejected, Samuel. It is not you who is being rejected. It is what you represent that is being rejected." What Samuel represents is the tradition of a people who have sought to center their lives on the God who brought them out of Egypt, who delivered them from the Philistines. What God tells Samuel is that Israel is rejecting its own center, its own identity. Israel is not rejecting Samuel. Israel is rejecting God.

God also tells Samuel something else. This desire for a king is nothing new for Israel. The rejection of God is nothing new. It continues a long history of the people of God seeking security at the price of freedom. "Ever since I brought them out of slavery in Egypt, they have wanted to go back there," God tells Samuel. Indeed, if we go back to Exodus to read the account of Israel's release from slavery, we will find that they are often dragged into freedom, kicking and screaming.

In chapter 14 of Exodus when Pharaoh's soldiers are pressing down on Israel, and Israel's back is to the sea, they are terrified. They cry out to Moses,

> *Was it because there were no graves in Egypt that you have taken us away to die in the wilderness? What have you done to us, bringing us out of Egypt? Is this not the very thing we told you in Egypt, "Let us alone and let us serve the Egyptians"? For it would have been better for us to serve the Egyptians than to die in the wilderness.* — Exodus 14:11-12

And then God delivers them by parting the sea, and Pharaoh's soldiers drown. They begin their journey to freedom, but they are hungry. They don't have any food. They cry out again to Moses,

> *If only we had died by the hand of the Lord in the land of Egypt, when we sat by the fleshpots and ate our fill*

of bread; for you have brought us out into this wilder-
ness to kill this whole assembly with hunger.
— Exodus 16:3

In Exodus chapter 22, while Moses is up on Mount Sinai receiving the law that will become Israel's guide, the people of Israel are making a golden calf to worship. Gold and money always seem to be rivals for God in our hearts, don't they? Whether we're in the wilderness 3,000 years ago or whether we're sitting in this congregation this morning, this rivalry remains strong.

Throughout the book of Judges, and as we have seen in 1 Samuel, the Israelites are trying to balance the worship of their God with the worship of the Canaanite gods. They do this not because they are so bad and evil. They do this because life can be so fierce; because the powers and principalities are so intimidating; because the people's anxieties are so high. Let us remember that the people ask Samuel for a king not because of a military threat, but because justice has been perverted. They want justice to be established. They believe that if they can get a king, then justice will be re-established. It is a naive belief on one level, but it is rooted in desperation. We must note that these are not mean, stubborn people, openly defying God. They are regular folks just like us, encountering the chaos of life, repelled by the injustice and corruption all around them. They're trying to find a little bit of stability in their lives. We have to be careful not to dehumanize or stereotype these folks as weak or mean or lusting for power and profit, especially considering how often Christians have done such stereotyping of Judaism. Israel remembers chapter 8 of 1 Samuel because it speaks to each generation, and it speaks to us.

God wants Samuel to make it clear to God's people the cost of this kind of step. They will get what they want. They will get a king. They will get a Pharaoh, but they will have to return to the slavery of Egypt in order to do it. Samuel lays it out for the people. It is a gruesome narrative characterizing the centralization of power in a king. The people's property will be taken. Their sons will be forced to serve in the army. Their daughters will be at the disposal of the king. Samuel ends his warning with difficult words. "You will sell yourselves back into slavery." And yet, despite this stern warning, the people cry out, "Give us a king!"

We now have to make a decision on how to interpret this story. These people are either incredibly stupid, or there is something else going on here, something that the authors of 1 Samuel want each generation to remember and to ponder. What the authors of 1 Samuel want us to know is that in each generation, and in each of us, there is this same struggle between wanting to live in Egypt and wanting to have God at the center of our lives. The authors of 1 Samuel are reminding us that we all seek to live between God and Egypt, and it is a difficult journey.

Our lives should be a circle with God at the center. Most often, though, our lives are an ellipse that has two centers, Egypt and God. We often try to live between these two centers. We spend our lives going back and forth, wanting to feel secure and yet wanting freedom, often seeking to answer our anxieties by selling ourselves back into slavery. But, we also want to continue to experience what Israel experienced, the God who calls them and pulls them back into freedom.

We see many signs of this process in our time. After the Civil Rights Movement of the 1950s and 1960s, with its emphasis on freedom and equality, for a couple of decades now we've had a movement to go back to Egypt. "Let's go back to the traditional values. We don't need the NAACP anymore. We don't need all this talk about freedom. Let's go back to a time when life was simpler, when everybody knew where his or her place was. Women knew their places back then. Poor people knew their places back then. Comfortable people knew their places back then. It was a time when black folk and gay and lesbian folk weren't in your faces. Let's go back to Egypt."

It reminds me of a *Garfield* comic strip. Garfield is a caped crusader, and he's got this mask on, and he breaks into a pet store. All of the animals are in cages, of course, and Garfield begins to open the doors of the cages, saying, "You're free! You're free!" But all the animals just sit there in the cages. Garfield ponders what to do for a while, and then he starts slamming the doors of the cages, saying, "You're safe! You're safe!" He goes out the door saying, "We aren't much into freedom these days."

This certainly seems to be true on a societal level. Like the people of Israel, we see injustice and corruption all around us, and we often want to move back into Egypt in order to deal with it. It also describes the struggle in our individual lives, how we seek to live between God and Egypt. Each of us has our own pain, our own struggles, and our own anxieties that bring us to worship today. We're each trying to work out our own journeys as we seek to live between Egypt and God. We want to answer our anxieties with a place that feels safe, but often our answer is a quick trip to slavery, causing us to lose touch with our center, which is God. Yet, God continues to call us and pull us toward freedom, toward our center, our true home, which is God.

We must all work out our own compromises on this journey. As Paul says, we must all work out our salvation with fear and trembling, and the focus of our work is in trying to live between Egypt and God. Our children were both on the safety patrol when they were in elementary school, and they often had to lead the Pledge of Allegiance. As their time of leadership approached, they came to me to discuss it. They wanted to discuss it because they had noticed at sporting events that I had not put my hand over my heart when the Pledge of Allegiance was said. After those sporting events, they asked me, "Daddy, why don't you put your hand over your heart like everyone else?" I replied that I didn't mind pledging allegiance to the nation but that my heart belonged to God. I also told them that I wanted them to remember that. When they got to be officers on the safety patrol, the problem emerged. They were supposed to lead the school in the pledge, and they were supposed to put their hands over their hearts. They now asked me, "What should we do?" I told them my preference. I preferred that they not put their hands over their hearts. Yet, I also told them that this would have to be their decision, which they would have to work out for themselves. This is what they came up with. They took their hands and put them *almost* on their hearts, not quite touching themselves. They managed to appear to put their hands on their hearts, all the while preserving their own sense of not quite giving total allegiance to the nation.

For me, it is a metaphor of how we all try to live between Egypt and God. We don't want to lose either center, so we try to keep them both. That's what my children tried to do on the safety patrol. That's what I try to do every day. That's what most of us try to do. That's what Israel tried to do. That's what we all find ourselves trying to do, living between Egypt and God.

Our passage today reminds us of this dilemma as we seek to live with these two centers of our lives. Israel remembers this passage not because it wants us to know how stupid its ancestors are, but rather because it wants us to know how human they are, how similar to us they are. It is a dilemma, this life with two centers. There are many benefits to living in Egypt. Indeed, Israel prospers under the monarchy. Saul drives back the Philistines and begins to set the borders. David, the second king, unites the nation and establishes Jerusalem as its center and its capital. Solomon, the son of David, has great economic development and builds the great temple that becomes the center of Judaism.

This passage also reminds us, however, that after those three kings, the nation falls apart and splits. It reminds Israel and us of the cost of living in Egypt. Israel moves away from its center, who is God, and moves back into slavery. This occurs first in its own midst under its own kings, who do just what Samuel said they would. Then Israel moves into exile and slavery in Babylon.

This passage gives us a stern warning about seeking to live between God and Egypt. Yet, for all its warning, this passage continues to remind us that God is in the midst of these people. It is God who says "Yes" to the monarchy. This passage, and the entire biblical story, points us to a fundamental fact of our lives, whether we live in Israel many thousands of years ago or whether we're here this morning. Though we try to live in Egypt, God will not let us alone. Though we try to push God from the center of our lives, God remains at the center. God will not leave us alone. God will not give up on us. We do sell ourselves into slavery in order to feel safe and secure, but God continues to call us back into freedom.

We put our toes into the waters of freedom. We put our toes into the waters of freedom for just a little while, then we run back to the safety of Egypt. But God continues to kindle our thirst, and we return to the waters of life, this time to put a knee in; then, sooner or later, to be immersed in the waters of life and freedom.

It will be a rugged journey for us, as we all know. The internal voices and pressures inside each of us and the voices of the principalities and the powers outside ourselves are powerful and scary. They ask us to accept the simplistic answers, answers in which a certain group of people make all the decisions, where the power is not distributed, where justice is interpreted to mean giving the powerful what they want. In a time like this, when people want simple answers, we're asked to remember that life is complex. In a time when folks want to set up enemies so that they can be blamed, we're asked to remember that we are those who are called to love people that we deem as enemies. In a time when we're told that society is collapsing because black folk have left their place, because women have left home, and because gay and lesbian persons have been affirmed just a little bit, we are called to remember that it is the rapacious appetite of a consumer society that sees all of life as a commodity, it is this appetite that is causing society to collapse. It is a time when we hear those voices in ourselves that tell us that we cannot trust God, that we must come on over to the idols of the world and find our way back to Egypt, then we must remember God's movement in our lives and listen for God's voice in our midst. It is the voice telling us that the only way we can find real safety and real security, the only way we can find life, is by touching the one who is at the center of our lives, the God we know in Jesus Christ.

These authors of 1 Samuel know what they are doing in this story when they include these ambivalent words about kingship in the sacred text of scripture. This story is as contemporary as this morning's newspaper, or in this electronic age, as today's e-mail. Israel sought to live between God and Egypt, and so do we. That's a curse for us, but it is also a blessing. God is part of our struggle and will not give up on us. The biblical promise is that God is in the midst of our struggle; that God will not give up on us. God continues to call us and pull us, as God pulled Israel, as God pulled the followers of Jesus. God continues to pull us, to call us into freedom, into life, into the center of our lives, who is the true God. Amen.

Slouching Toward Bethlehem
1 Samuel 16:1-13
August 30, 1998

In the famous Christmas carol by Phillips Brooks, we see a little town awaiting the birth of a Savior. "O little town of Bethlehem, how still we see thee lie. Above thy deep and dreamless sleep, the silent stars go by."[1] But in today's passage in 1 Samuel, we see a grim picture of Bethlehem. As Bethlehem waits in this story, there is grief and confusion and feelings of loss all around. To borrow a line from the Irish poet William Butler Yeats, Samuel "slouches toward Bethlehem."[2]

Samuel is grieving. He and his line of leadership have been rejected by the people of Israel, who want a king. And Saul, the king whom Samuel selected under God's direction, has now been rejected by God. Israel is now in limbo. It has a king who still reigns but who has been rejected by God. Samuel goes back to Ramah, grieving over Saul and over Israel. Indeed, he sees no future for Israel. Samuel grieves over the kingship, which he did not want in the first place, over the king who did not want to become king and who has now been rejected as king by God. Samuel grieves over the shortsightedness of the people of Israel who rejected God and wanted a king. And now, God has rejected that very king, Saul. What is going on? What will happen? Is all lost?

In the midst of this grief and despair comes the power of God. God tells Samuel, "Get up. There's work to be done. I've already got a new king picked out." Samuel is less than enthusiastic. He has been through this with God before. In the present circumstances, Samuel's grief and despair make him see disaster everywhere. There is no good news. Not even God can turn this situation around. When God tells Samuel to get up and get going, Samuel digs in his heels. "I won't go! How can I go to Bethlehem and anoint a new king? If Saul, the current king — the king you chose, the king you rejected — hears about it, he will kill me."

45

It is an interesting shift in Samuel. Up until now in the book of 1 Samuel, he has been a fierce warrior-prophet who has hounded and tormented Saul as king. He has never been afraid of Saul. But now, when God orders him to Bethlehem, he trembles in fear. His knees are knocking. "I can't go down there!" Samuel sees no hope. In his grief and sadness, his fear has gotten the best of him. He resists God's invitation to go to Bethlehem. God offers him a way out. "You're a circuit-riding preacher, aren't you? Just go down to Bethlehem and have a revival. Pitch your tent, invite everybody in, and give Jesse a special invitation — Jesse and his sons." Samuel does what God commands him to do. He reluctantly slouches toward Bethlehem. He doesn't go to Bethlehem full of joy and anticipation. Finally, God is moving. There's going to be renewal in Israel, a great revival that begins in Bethlehem! No, Samuel doesn't go to Bethlehem in this frame of mind. He slouches to Bethlehem, full of fear and dread of what will happen.

The authors of this story in 1 Samuel well understand what it means to be a human being, and they emphasize it in this passage. The authors want us to note here that even the great Samuel had struggles. We must recall the esteem in which Samuel is held. The biblical books that contain the stories of the great king, David, are not called 1 and 2 David — they are called 1 and 2 Samuel in the Hebrew Scriptures. Samuel commands great respect in the memory of Israel, but here the authors emphasize the struggles in his heart. Here, on the way to Bethlehem, Samuel is in turmoil, and he slouches toward Bethlehem. We see a humorous story of Samuel's entry into the little town of Bethlehem. He is fearful, looking over his shoulder for the spies of Saul who may hear what he is going to Bethlehem to do. In the town of Bethlehem itself, the elders hear that the powerful and dangerous Samuel is approaching their town. They do not know that Samuel's knees are knocking. They only know the fierce warrior-prophet who has served God so well and who has so recently hacked King Agag to death in chapter 15. This Samuel is coming to Bethlehem. They, too, come out in fear to meet Samuel. "Do you come in peace?" They ask it with hope and prayer. We have, then, a comic scene of a proud warrior slouching toward Bethlehem, trembling in fear, knees knocking. The elders come out to greet him. They are trembling, and their knees are knocking, bumbling, filled with fear, taking one step forward and two steps backward.

And there are even more surprises for Samuel when he arrives. Not only is God sending him to this hick town, to this little place in Judah, but things don't go well, either. The sons of Jesse are paraded before Samuel, and as each one passes before him, he expects to feel God's Spirit. "This is the one. Look how tall he is!" Now, I understand why that one was rejected. I don't know why the others were rejected, but it makes sense to a short guy like me why the tall Eliab was rejected. No, he's not the one. Then Abinadab — no, he's not the one. Then Shammah — no, he's not the one. Then four more sons are brought before Samuel and inspected and rejected. None of them is the one. Nothing happens. All of the sons of Jesse are paraded before Samuel, and nothing happens. There is no voice from God telling Samuel that this is the one. Samuel is wondering, "What is happening? Does God know what he is doing? Have I risked my life coming down to this little town for nothing?"

In desperation Samuel asks Jesse, "Are there any sons left?" "Well, yes, there's a little boy out there, tending the sheep, but he doesn't belong in this lottery for the kingship. He's too young. He's just a boy." Samuel orders that the young boy be brought before him, and he is astonished to feel God's Spirit when he sees this shepherd boy. "This is the one — get up and anoint him!" "This is the one? God, you have got to be kidding; a little shepherd boy — king of Israel?" Not even the clever and battle-hardened Samuel is ready for this. Samuel undoubtedly believes that God has lost his mind, but he follows God's Spirit. He anoints a young boy as king of Israel, a boy named David.

The authors of 1 Samuel want us to remember that it is not Samuel who saves Israel. It is not Moses who saves Israel. It is not Deborah who saves Israel. It is not even David who saves Israel. It is God, who is moving in these kinds of vessels, who saves Israel. God's choice for the next king of Israel emphasizes Israel's dependency upon God. A mere child is chosen to be king, a child who will have to be nurtured and protected and taught. No strong warrior like Eliab, no powerful son like Abinadab, but rather a little shepherd boy named David, who will have to be protected and taught by God and, yes, by Samuel. It is the clearest sign yet that the destiny of Israel is not in Samuel's hands, not in Saul's hands, not in David's hands. Israel's destiny is in God's hands.

Samuel slouches toward Bethlehem and finds astonishing news. I understand his fear and reluctance well. As I was reading this story in chapter 16 of 1 Samuel, I was reminded of my first pastorate with my wife in a small church. A couple of weeks after we came to be pastors there, we had our first session meeting. Toward the end of the meeting, the elders told us that there was something that we needed to know. They indicated that they were fairly certain that the church treasurer had been embezzling money from the church. They had discovered it several months earlier but were waiting on us to arrive in order to solve it.

We made plans to go to the treasurer's home to discuss it. The treasurer was an elder who had rotated off the Session, and his wife was actively involved in the church. I saw disaster looming before me. The church had only twelve members anyway, and if we lost two of them, we weren't going to be in good shape. I dreaded going out to see him. I put off calling him for a couple of days, and finally, I made the call, not telling him the purpose of the visit. I was mad at the elders for not taking care of it before we arrived. Here I was an inexperienced minister, and I was being thrown into the fire that could devour this little church, and perhaps more to the point of my fear, could devour me. I was filled with fear and dread and anger. I was physically ill the night before we went to visit him.

When we got to his house, we had a time of chatting and getting acquainted. As we talked, I learned that he was an avid hunter. And, as we talked, I looked around the room, and I noticed shotguns and crossbows and rifles hanging on the walls. I can tell from your laughter that you have already discerned what I was imagining. I said, "O God, save me!" My knees were knocking, my heart was pounding, and my voice was trembling. Finally, I brought up the purpose of our visit and the subject of the money. And God did save us. God did redeem the moment. The treasurer admitted his guilt, seeing this as an opportunity to stop the madness and lift up his errors. He admitted his guilt, and he made restitution to the church, and he stayed in the church.

I was stunned that evening and stunned throughout the process. God had moved through my wife and me. We were not eager vessels for God's action. We were not enthusiastic, ready to go out and convict the sinner, ready to witness for Jesus. We were reluctant, grumpy, and scared, slouching toward the treasurer's house. Yet, God acted through us. God redeemed the moment. Not because of us — we obviously were not ready or eager vessels — but rather through us.

I think this is the point of the story of chapter 16 of 1 Samuel, the story of the transition from Samuel to Saul to David. This whole saga is grounded in the power and initiative and the surprises of God. It affirms, it asserts — indeed, it demands — that we hear that God is working in our lives. Not always when we're fierce and fight for justice, not always when we're ready to go out and save the world, but in the midst of our struggles. God is working in us. Our task, then, is not to make ourselves perfect. Samuel was far from perfect. He was discouraged and grieving. He did not want to go to Bethlehem. He tried to get out of going, but he finally went.

As the story of Samuel demonstrates, we are often weak vessels for God. Paradoxically, it is our strength that sometimes causes the problem. It's often our strength that makes us weak. It's the idea that we know the answer, that we always know what should be done, as Samuel thought he knew. His fierceness and his dedication got in the way on the road to Bethlehem, and he had to work himself up to responding to God's leading. He goes down to Bethlehem, not full of hope and joy. He goes full of dread, slouching toward Bethlehem, the city of David and the city of Jesus.

God uses Samuel, grump that he is. This story reminds us that whether we're open vessels, listening for God, ready and eager to serve God, or whether we're stubborn and resentful and can't believe that God wants this kind of movement, there is a promise. This story reminds us of the promise of the biblical witness, a promise that is both comforting and terrifying. God *is* in our midst, lifting us, pulling us, comforting us, not always taking us where we want to go. God would not leave Israel alone. God would not leave Samuel alone. God will not leave us alone.

It is not always good news that God will not leave us alone. We often resist it, as Samuel did, as he slouched toward Bethlehem. The promise of this story — indeed, the promise of the entire biblical witness — is that God has claimed us and will not desert us. God will reshape us whether we're grumpy or open, whether we're willing to follow, or running the other way. God *will* make us God's people. Amen.

----

1. "O Little Town Of Bethlehem," Phillips Brooks, in *The Presbyterian Hymnal* (Louisville, Kentucky: Westminster/John Knox Press, 1990), p. 43.

2. "The Second Coming," *Selected Poems and Two Plays of William Butler Yeats,* ed. M. L. Rosenthal (New York: Collier Books, 1962), p. 91.

Battling The Idols

In this series on Romans, Stroupe re-examines the nature of the Christian life in the context of Paul's language of flesh and spirit. In reflecting upon Paul's distinctive use of these terms, Stroupe offers a corrective to what, for many, is the familiar Christian vision of both the predicament of sin and the liberation from that predicament made possible by Jesus Christ. Stroupe's corrective proves to be more robust on both counts. The life of the Spirit described here entails a radical re-orientation of our whole being to the new reality of freedom in Jesus Christ. For Stroupe, this re-orientation may have more to do with firing our passion and imagination than with strengthening our will. Like the struggle of Israel's journey with the living God, and the struggle of responding to the gospel's call for justice, the Christian life is marked by the continual struggle in our hearts between the apparent security provided by the idols of the world and the risky adventure of freedom in Jesus Christ.

Identities And Idols
Romans 7:14-25
September 27, 1998

"How come I can make good decisions in a boxing ring but not in my life?" That was the lead story in Tuesday's sports section in *The Atlanta Constitution*.[1] Some of you may not read the sports section, but I do. It was the story of boxing champion Evander Holyfield's revelation that he had fathered three children by three different women in the last year, one of whom is his wife. "How come I can make good decisions in a boxing ring but not in my life?" Holyfield's question goes to the heart of the struggle that Paul lifts up in these verses in chapter 7 of Romans: "I do not understand my own actions, for I do not do what I want to do, but I do the very thing I hate."

Now, obviously Evander Holyfield is not an undisciplined man. Anyone who has a body like his and who boxes for a living has a strong will. If you are going to stand there and let someone hit you in the face, that takes discipline and a strong will. Holyfield's story is thus not about his weak will. Rather, Holyfield's story, and Paul's words in Romans, remind us of the limits of the human will rather than of its weakness. How many times do we hurt ourselves or hurt others and then say, "I really didn't mean to do that," or, "I can't believe I did that!" Paul's words in Romans 7 point us to the deeper issue beyond the human will. It is an issue that involves our entire identity, not just our will.

Paul is seeking to come to terms with this identity and with this process in these verses. The truth is that we know what is right on some levels, but we cannot always will to do it. All of us have the experience of having made decisions that almost seem to come from another person in us, another power inside ourselves that seems determined to have us hurt ourselves or hurt others. It is a power that is part of us on the one hand, but seems beyond our control at times. Paul uses a vivid image to describe this. He is at war with himself, at war with parts of his own self.

53

Paul seeks to help us understand this struggle and to help us work through it.

In order to try to work through Paul's efforts in this area, we're going to have to define some of his terms. The first term is "law." What Paul means by "law" is not the legal system where violations bring public censure or prison. What he means by "law" is the guiding principles of our lives, those precepts and norms that keep us grounded and that keep us focused on what we should be doing. The concept of law for Paul is deep and profound. It is the moral values that we are taught as children and as adults. The Ten Commandments are part of this law, as are the two great commandments from Jesus. The law for Paul is the set of principles that guide us, especially when we are at war with ourselves. In those instances when we can't figure out what to do, we should turn to the law to guide us.

The problem for Paul is that he knows that while the law can reign us in and guide us, it can't deliver us to God. He also knows that there are many "laws," many cultural contexts. Part of the problem with the law is that it is always rooted in cultural context. For example, one of the guiding moral values of American culture is that money brings life. That's one of our laws. That's what we believe. If you want to be somebody in this culture, you must get some money. We are beginning to see, though, that moral value is destructive to human life and is leading to a breakdown in community that we all regret.

The problem that Paul raises in regard to the law is not that we fail to teach moral values. That's not our problem, though conservatives say this all the time. You hear Dr. Laura on the radio saying that we don't teach values. We teach values every day in this country, and one of them is the moral value of money. It's a flawed value, a flawed law — that's the problem. It's not that we don't teach values. We continue to teach values and the law. The values that we teach, though, bring us to the point of destruction. As Paul puts it, it is at this point that the law loses its power to redeem us. Obedience to the law in this case doesn't bring life. It brings death. The law ultimately loses its power to redeem because it's always rooted in cultural context and in the flesh.

54

That brings us to the second term that we must define — "flesh," that wonderful word that has mystified us and scared us and inflamed us. When Paul uses the word "flesh," he is not confining it to the body or to sexuality. That's how we often interpret the word flesh in the church, to mean "the body" or "sexuality." It's easy to do that these days with Evander Holyfield and Bill Clinton running around. But that's not what Paul means by "flesh." Where Paul talks about "flesh," he is talking about the struggles in our historic existence as people, people who have been raised and taught by others in a cultural context, our historic existence as cultures and community. He is talking about our existence that is dominated by the powers of the world.

"Flesh," for Paul, is the process by which we seek to find our way in the world, to try to answer the questions of our existence, the questions that are at the center of our lives. The question of our finitude, for example. How do we deal with the fact that we know that we are going to die? Dealing with this question is one of the central ways that we order our lives. And what do we do with our sense of individuality, the fact that we know that we are separate, the fact that there is this longing in us to go home, to be connected? What do we do with the anxiety that both of these raise, our finitude and our individuality? Paul suggests that all cultures and all contexts come to deal with life in ways that seek to answer these questions, and all the answers are flawed.

The idols of the world move into our cultural answers and move into our individual answers in order to help us assuage our anxieties, to help us deal with our fear of death and our fear of life, and to help us feel like we belong. If we just buy the right product, we will belong. That is one of the fundamental ways that the questions of finitude and individuality are answered by the laws of American culture. Just buy the product! That's what Paul means by "flesh." The flesh answers our anxieties. "Buy the product, and you will belong." The flesh enables us to push that anxiety back from our consciousness. That's what Paul means by "flesh" — not the body, not sex, but rather our whole way of answering the questions of life. Later on in this series on Romans, I'll seek to flesh out Paul's concept of "flesh" more thoroughly, but for today, I want us to hear clearly that "flesh" is more than the body or sexuality. It is the process by which we come to accept the cultural answers to the questions that are at the heart of our lives.

One more term, "sin." Another term that the church loves to talk about. My wife says that I love sin more than anything else. I'm not quite sure what she means by that, but ... I do like to talk about sin. I will admit that much. For Paul, sin is not so much an act or an action as it is a whole orientation toward reality. For Paul, sin is not just an act like stealing or lying. For Paul, the act is a symptom of sin, like pain is a symptom of problems in our bodies. From Paul's view, the action is a symptom of a whole system of understanding ourselves and understanding the world. Sin is that state of being alienated from the center of our lives, the God we know in Jesus Christ. Sometimes we are conscious of this alienation from God. There are moments in our lives when we are acutely aware of how far we have distanced ourselves from God. Paul certainly seems to be aware of his alienation in these verses for today. "Wretched man that I am! Who will deliver me from this process of death?" Sometimes, however, we are not aware of our alienation from God. Sometimes our identity is so intertwined with the idols of the world that we are not conscious of our alienation. It's a given premise in this culture that money brings life. It is accepted by all political spectrums, and we are not aware how alienated we are because of the acceptance of this belief. For Paul, it is this understanding, this orientation toward reality, that is sin, and it is true for both individuals and communities.

Now that we've given some brief definitions of Paul's terms, how does it all work in this difficult passage? Difficult as this passage is, it has a profundity to it that we all understand. "I do what I don't want to do, and I can't seem to do what I want to do." I don't believe that there is any one of us in this congregation today who does not understand this kind of struggle in our lives. How does Paul put this together so that we can understand our profound difficulty and complexity? Paul emphasizes the extent into which we are sold into sin. He says, "Now if I do what I do not want to do, it is no longer I who does it but sin which dwells within me." The popular translation of this is often, "The devil made me do it." In this approach, Paul emphasizes the complexity of sinfulness. It's not just a matter of the will. Evander Holyfield says, "I can make good decisions in the boxing ring. I cannot make good decisions in my personal life. Why not?" Paul would answer that the issue is not just what Holyfield is *doing*; it is also a matter of how he is perceiving, how he is thinking, how he is feeling. The roots of his actions are there. Paul wants us to understand that sin is not just a matter of the will. Rather, sin is a matter of how we perceive ourselves and the world, and how we perceive others. It is a whole orientation toward life, an orientation rooted in brokenness and alienation.

It is complex because we have received this orientation long before we knew anything about receiving it. Long before we had any idea that we were receiving this way of viewing the world. It was taught to us by people we trust and love, our mommas and our daddies, our grandparents, our teachers, and our preachers. They were teaching us many good ways of living in the world, but they were also teaching us ways that were rooted in brokenness. They were not consciously teaching us the ways of brokenness, and the reason they were not teaching us in this manner is not because they were bad but because they, too, struggled with alienation, with trying to come to terms with idolatry in their lives. We teach our children well. We teach them this whole system of how to come to terms with the questions of finitude and individuality and anxiety. I think this process is what is at the heart of the idea of original sin, that we receive this whole system of idolatry into ourselves long before we know it.

I want to offer some examples of this process. Sometimes it is a struggle with the law. What does the Tenth Commandment emphasize? Who knows what the Tenth Commandment is? Thou shall not covet. For all of you out in the congregation who don't believe that we need to come to Sunday school, please note this mini-quiz. The Tenth Commandment emphasizes, "Thou shall not covet." But our whole global economy is now driven by cultivating covetousness. It cultivates the desire in each of us and in all of us to want more and more stuff. We're not motivated just by our need to eat, but by our desire to eat *certain kinds* of food. We're not driven by just needing shelter, but by our desire for a *certain kind* of housing. We're not driven just by the need for clothing but by our desire for a *certain kind* of clothing. It is the way our entire economy is driven.

I heard a report this week on National Public Radio about Japan's economic woes. It emphasized that the way that Japan will get out of its economic crisis is for its people to start consuming more stuff. If they would just start consuming more, then Japan's economic woes would end. To have the people of Japan accept the idolatrous definition that they are primarily consumers is the proposed answer to Japan's economic difficulties. In this sense, our whole way of life is at odds with the Tenth Commandment, and we teach this to our children, having accepted it ourselves because it has been taught to us.

A second example is the continuing power of racism. I was leading a workshop on racism last weekend in a Presbytery in North Carolina, and both black and white folk were in the workshop. As we went around the room and talked about race and its impact on our lives, almost every white person there talked about learning racism from people that they loved and trusted. "My mother taught me racism." "My Sunday school teacher taught me racism." "Everybody just knew that blacks were inferior." People they trusted taught them racism, and so it wasn't only a matter of the will. It was a matter of having to come to terms with their whole history and their heritage, a history that had also given them many good values. The white folk also talked about their current struggles with racism. They would be driving down the road and a black person would cut in front of them, and racism would just pop into their consciousness. They couldn't believe it. They were ashamed and shocked, but there it was. It was so ingrained that it almost seemed beyond their will to control. That is what Paul is talking about here in this passage in Romans, the power of sinfulness that is deeply rooted in who we are; the power of sinfulness that we learn, not from mean people, but from good people.

Here is one more example, an example that lifts up the cultural context of the law. I'll give you one more chance on the Ten Commandments. What is the Seventh Commandment? It's very much on everybody's mind these days in the United States with the sex scandal in the White House. Yes. "Thou shalt not commit adultery." All right, you're doing better. That sounds straightforward, doesn't it? If you're married, you shouldn't have sexual relations with anyone except your spouse. The problem is that this is not the Old Testament definition of adultery. The Old Testament definition of adultery does not refer to a married person having sex outside of marriage. The Old Testament definition of adultery refers to a man having sex with a married woman who is not his wife. The Seventh Commandment permits a married man to have sex with women other than his wife, as long as the other women are unmarried. If a married man has sex with a single woman, he is not committing adultery according to the Seventh Commandment. The original context of the Seventh Commandment, then, is not about how we married men relate to *our* wives. It is about how we relate to other men's wives. Now we can see more clearly how the Seventh Commandment functioned in its original context. It was a property law, a law about women as property of men, not as marriage partners. It is a law about how property is to be treated. Women who belong to men as wives are not to be violated by other men. Women, then, are seen as property of their husbands, and not as marriage partners.

Christians no longer understand the Seventh Commandment in this way. We now see adultery as a two-way street, affecting both husbands and wives. This change was made because Jesus came along and radicalized this Seventh Commandment. Jesus knew that this Seventh Commandment had not addressed the humanity of women, that it had continued the cultural context in which women had no rights or dignity. Jesus said these words about the Seventh Commandment in his Sermon on the Mount, in Matthew 5. "You have heard that it was said, 'You shall not commit adultery.' But I say to you that everyone who looks at a woman with lust has already committed adultery with her in his heart."

Jesus deepens and radicalizes this Seventh Commandment. Women are not sex objects for men. Women are not property of men. Jesus is affirming the worth and dignity of women as human beings, regardless of their relationship to men. Jesus is reminding us that we have to be very careful how we use this Seventh Commandment. It is Jesus taking us into the territory that Paul is describing in chapter 7 in Romans. That territory is our culturally determined view of women that leads to adultery, the idea that women exist to satisfy men. Jimmy Carter touched on this struggle in his famous *Playboy* interview in 1976 when he admitted that he lusted after women other than his wife. In light of what's going on in Washington these days, this sounds pretty tame. Back then, though, it caused an uproar for Jimmy Carter to admit that he had been raised in a culture that saw women as sex objects. He was pointing to the deep and complex roots of sinfulness. It was not so much how weak his will was. It was that his heart had been taught in a certain way about what women are; a belief that he has been taught and a belief that he has to unlearn.

This gets us to the central point of Paul's emphasis here. Sinfulness is complex. It's not just a matter of saying, "I will not do it again," although, that is certainly part of it. It's not just a matter of overt acts, but of attitudes of the heart way beyond the reach of the will. It is in this struggle that Paul emphasizes the extent to which "the devil made me do it." Paul puts it like this. "The sin that dwells within me" made me do it. That sin is not a demon or a devil that takes over our personality, but rather, the very way we learn and develop as human beings. We *learn* these definitions of racism, of women being sex objects, of money being the answer. We learn these long before we have the capacity to resist them, and we learn them from people we trust. By the time our sinfulness is revealed to us, by the time it comes to our consciousness, it is already so intertwined with our understanding of ourselves that it is very difficult to eradicate.

This is the struggle that Paul is articulating in these verses in Romans. It is not just a matter of willpower or repression. He's talking about a whole reorientation to reality, a change to our entire perceptual apparatus. It's what Jesus meant in John's Gospel when he told Nicodemus that he had to be born again in order to come into the God movement. Jesus didn't mean that we have to have a dramatic conversion experience. He meant that we would have to be radically re-oriented in the way we see ourselves and the way we see the world — a very difficult process.

No one understands this better or writes more profoundly about it than Paul. He is at war with himself, and in his most despairing moments, he cries out, "Wretched man that I am! Who will deliver me from this process of death?" How will we get delivered? How will we get out of this war? Paul suggests the answer in the very next verse after his lament of despair. "Thanks be to God through Jesus Christ our Lord!"

We are going to be looking at this answer more fully in the weeks ahead, but let us note here that Paul suggests that the answer to this struggle — this profound struggle that is in each of our hearts — is to hear a new story about ourselves, about reality, to hear a new story about life itself and about what is at the center of life. A new story in the life and death and resurrection of Jesus Christ. We need to begin to let that story become part of our story.

For the rest of this series in Romans, we'll be talking about this process of beginning to hear a new story, of beginning to appropriate that new story in our lives. Whether we've heard this story 1,000 times, as many of us have, or whether we're hearing it this morning for the first time, there are always places in our hearts for us to discover and to celebrate the good news. "Thanks be to God through Jesus Christ our Lord!" Lord, you have known us and examined us. Long before we speak, long before they come up to our consciousness, you know our thoughts. My paraphrase of Psalm 139 reminds us that our relationship to God is not a question of what we know. It is a question of what God knows. Paul understands the struggles in our hearts, and he lifts those up. And, he gives thanks that even as God knows that struggle, he says, "Yes." "Thanks be to God through Jesus Christ our Lord!" Amen.

---

1. Jeff Schultz, "Infidelity Is Holyfield's Toughest Foe," *Atlanta Constitution,* September 22, 1998, p. F-1.

Flesh And Spirit
Romans 8:1-17
October 18, 1998

Flesh and spirit. In these verses Paul develops a strong contrast between these two ways of life. He puts it like this.

> *For those who live according to the flesh set their minds on the things of the flesh, but those who live according to the Spirit set their minds on the things of the Spirit. To set the mind on the flesh is death, but to set the mind on the Spirit is life and peace.*
> — Romans 8:5-6

Paul has a profound point here, but we often miss that point in the church, for we usually misunderstand what he means by "flesh" and "spirit." I want to take some time this morning to look at the meaning of these words and what Paul means when he is using them.

For many of us, when we hear the word "flesh," we think of the body and especially of sexuality. Given our current national crisis over the Clinton presidency, it's not surprising that we might connect flesh with sexuality. That's understandable. Sexuality is part of the flesh. But, Paul's concept of flesh goes far beyond sexuality and far beyond the body. Flesh and sexuality have been connected in the church for a long time. The strongest connection was made by the most influential theologian in the history of the church since Paul. He was an African named Augustine, and he wrote about 400 C.E. He connected sinfulness with sexuality. He asserted that original sin was passed from one generation to the next through sexual intercourse. Ever since then, Christians have tended to portray sinfulness in its most powerful form as sexuality, and thus flesh and sex have become synonymous. The church spends hours and hours debating about sexuality because we have connected it with flesh.

For Paul, however, flesh is not just the body or sexuality. Flesh certainly encompasses those, but it is so much more. For Paul, flesh is a whole way of being oriented toward life. For Paul, flesh describes that process by which we seek to answer the anxieties of our lives — as individuals, as communities — by turning to the idols of the world. For Paul, flesh really is a process. It describes the human response to our historical existence, a response in which we cling to the idols of the world in order to ease our anxiety. Paul notes that this process begins in us as individuals long before we know anything about it. It is passed on to us through the culture in which we live.

How does this really work? What is Paul talking about? How do we end up in the place where we prefer to rely on the idols of the world rather than God? Part of it is rooted in our being creatures. We have an awareness of our finitude and our mortality and our dependence. We know that we are going to get sick. We know that we have pain in our bodies and in our hearts. We know that we're going to die. We are aware of our dependency. We don't choose when we come into the world, and unless we commit suicide, we don't control when we leave the world. We don't have control over these central parts of our journeys. There is a deep, primordial awareness in our consciousness and in our whole being that we are not in control, that we are dependent, that we are creatures.

We are also aware that we are individuals, that we are separated on a profound level from every other person, from every other being in the universe. We have an individual consciousness, and we are aware that no one can ever come into ourselves as deeply as we might wish. We are aware of the deep struggle to know others and to be known by others. We are aware of how separated we are. In the first stages of the discovery of this separation, it is terrifying. We witness this awareness every Sunday in our nursery, when a young baby is left there while the parents come up to worship. Almost always, the baby ends up crying for its parents. The baby is aware of the separation and is not certain that it can survive. My wife and I experienced this with our son when he was less than a year old in Nashville, where I was interim pastor at Second Church. The nursery was right under the sanctuary and our son cried a lot in the nursery. You can imagine the scene for us as parents in worship. Rather than rejoicing in the music and worship as we have done this morning, as I got up to preach, I cringed as I heard my son screaming from the nursery underneath. It evoked in me a sense of guilt and inadequacy, because it touched a voice deep inside me, a voice that told me that I, too, was cut off and felt separated from the source of life.

We must not hear that this sense of dependency and of separation is bad in itself. Indeed, it is part of God's created order for us. We're supposed to be dependent. We're supposed to be separated as individuals, as people with an individual consciousness. God intends that we take these two poles of separation and dependency and weave them into a network where our individuality and our community are both affirmed. God has made us so that we belong to God and to one another, so that we are dependent on God and on one another. God has made us so that in order for us to survive from infancy, we must be nurtured by somebody. We can't feed ourselves when we're born. Somebody has to feed us. Somebody has to wipe our rear ends when we're little. We can't take care of ourselves. That happens to all of us. There are no exceptions. We are aware of this process, but we forget it. God means for us to belong to one another. We are to nurture one another, take care of one another, and help one another to grow.

We flee from that created order in our culture. One of the current crises in our culture is that people are living longer and growing more feeble due to the lengthening of the aging process. Many of us who are aging in this way — and many of our children — don't want to admit that sooner or later, someone is going to have to take care of us again. We thought we had gotten out of that stage when we left infancy and passed through adolescence. But we face a crisis now because many of us will live long enough to return to the stage where someone else will have to take care of us, and we hate that knowledge. That's why few institutions have been developed in our culture to respond to this situation. We have this awareness, and we are in flight from it.

We have taken God's created order and made it a problem. We have allowed our awareness of a sense of dependency to be seen as weakness. In this culture, if you are dependent, you are seen as weak, as less than worthy. We have allowed our individual consciousness to become alienated, and we are dominated by a sense that we are lost and lonely, never to find our home. Paul wants us to understand that this sense of lostness, of alienation, permeates our existence as individuals and as communities. We learn this process of feeling lost, of being in flight from God and from ourselves. We learn this process long before we are aware of it.

I learned racism long before I had any idea that I was learning it. I learned that black people were not human beings like myself, and I learned it from many good and decent people, including my family and my church, when I was a boy. I learned it from good and decent people who had learned it from good and decent people who had learned it from good and decent people. This is what Paul means by flesh. It is the process by which we learn — a process which ultimately we accept and make our own — to turn to the idols of the world in order to deal with our dependence and our separation, in order to deal with our fear and our anxiety.

I want to share a few more examples. The first is one that many of us wrestle with a lot: money and materialism. The church talks about sexuality all the time, but Jesus rarely ever talks about it. Jesus talks about money and its power in our lives all the time, but the church rarely ever talks about it. In our culture, money has the capacity to make us believe that we are answering that question of dependence. We may be dependent and separate and anxious about this condition, but if we can just get enough money, we can convince ourselves that we don't need anybody. We can answer the anxiety created by our dependence by seeking to obtain enough money so that we can fool ourselves into believing that we don't need anybody. We hear this all the time now in our culture. People are being told to pile up their money for retirement, because we are well aware that our culture has few institutions that emphasize the necessity and the joy of taking care of one another. So we're all trying to make that money, listening to the stock market every minute, and we become convinced that economic independence is the ultimate reality.

Paul calls this process flesh, the process by which we are in flight from God and from ourselves, running into the arms of the idols that convince us that dependency is a weakness, a liability. This process produces a culture like ours that is driven by materialism and money, where the goal of life is to get enough *stuff* so that we won't need anyone. The results are obvious. We live in a society where property is much more important than people. How can Christians not stand against such an idea? Jesus again and again and again emphasizes that people are much more valuable than property, yet we allow ourselves to believe that our culture is correct when it says that property is ultimate. We live in a culture where comfortable people like ourselves end up exploiting people who are poor so that we can extract wealth from their labor, all in order to get enough *stuff* so that we'll feel comfortable and can convince ourselves that we don't need anyone. It is a culture in which people who are poor are made to feel as if they are nobody, as if there is something wrong with them because they are poor. They are depicted as lazy or unintelligent, they simply don't understand how life works. They are blamed and demeaned for being dependent. It is this process that Paul is describing when he talks about flesh.

One more example. I can't mention sexuality without talking about it. It is the church's favorite example of sinfulness, not just in this century but also throughout our history as the body of Christ. Whenever we want to offer examples of sin, we usually end up talking about sex. It is clear that sexuality is a gift from God. It is a force that drives us out of ourselves to be in relationships with others, not so much to have intercourse, but as the simple need to touch and be touched. That's sexuality. The need and the desire to encounter others. Sexuality drives us out of the idolatrous belief that we can be on our own, that we can survive on our own. It helps us to understand that dependence is acceptable, and it shows us a way to legitimately overcome the loneliness of our individual consciousness by being related to others, not just as lovers, but also as friends and colleagues and neighbors and parents and children and grandparents.

This force hits us most clearly and most strongly in adolescence, when the hormones begin to rage, telling us that we need to separate from our parents and move toward our peers. That is part of God's created order. I would like for my children to think like I think and believe what I believe, but I know that I am also teaching them things — some of which I'm not even aware — that they will have to overcome. It's frightening to me, but that's the way this process of flesh works. I am communicating and teaching values to my children, some of which are helpful and some of which are harmful. But at the heart of adolescence is this drive to say, "I'm my own person," and sexuality is an essential part of that process. Think about this process, a process through which we all have passed or will pass. We go from infants who cry when our parents leave us to teenagers who rage when our parents ask us what time we're coming in. All of us who have teenagers, all of us have been teenagers, all of us who are teenagers, know that this is not an easy process. It is a necessary process, though, as we develop our own individual consciousness, and as we discern that God can speak through people other than our parents. Our growing awareness of our own sexuality is an important part of this process.

In a culture like ours that sees sexuality not as a gift but as a way to sell products, this passage through adolescence is made very difficult. Everywhere we look, everywhere we read, sexuality is being used as a way to sell products. Why? Because we've got to get that money. We worship the money. We take this powerful gift from God and turn it into a way to make more money. Boys and girls as pre-teens learn that the only real expression of sexuality is sexual intercourse. Teenage boys come to adolescence with the belief that sexual intercourse is ultimate, with their hormones reinforcing that only genital intercourse is the most intimate form of love and the highest expression of manhood. So he pressures the girlfriend to have sex with him, telling her that she doesn't love him unless she will have sex with him. Boys do this not just because they are manipulative, but also because, at a deeper level, they have been taught that this is true, that sexual intercourse is everything and is, indeed, the only thing.

Teenage girls, as we heard in our previous readings, are taught by our culture that they are property of men, that their purpose in life is to please men, that sexual intercourse is the way to please men. So teenage girls have tremendous internal pressure — not just pressure from their boyfriends — but internal pressure from the belief system that we have taught them. This pressure tells them to have sex with their boyfriends long before they're ready. In order to affirm their developing sense of self, in order to be somebody, teenage girls come to believe that they must have sex with their boyfriends. How many women and girls are being abused sexually and beaten up by their husbands and other men because we have taught them that their goal in life is to please men? It is what Paul means when he talks about flesh.

Flesh certainly includes the body and sexuality, but as we can see, it is much, much more. It is the flight into idolatry. This process permeates our laws and our consciousness and our bank accounts and our bodies. For Paul, "life according to the flesh" is the process by which we answer our anxieties as human beings by turning away from our true calling as children of God and turning toward the idols of the world. We must note that though it involves the human will, it is much more than the will, much deeper than the will. We learn this process long before we know about it, and it becomes intertwined with our very self-definition. That's why the church as a community of faith is so important. The church must be a place where we unlearn these idolatrous definitions of self and world, where we learn that women and men belong to God as equal partners, where we learn that people of all colors belong to God, that people of all economic classes belong to God. That is what the church is about, to help us learn what it means to be a child of God.

"Life according to the flesh" is powerful and overwhelming. Are we totally depraved, powerless, unable to know life, unable to know who we are, unable to know who God is? Paul says, on our own, "Yes." Yes, we are powerless on our own, because the idolatrous definitions are so blended with our self-definitions that we cannot even *imagine* a different definition. Paul suggests an alternative, the alternative that life is possible in the Spirit, in the life we have through the God we know in Jesus Christ. Paul lifts up the good news at the beginning of the eighth chapter of Romans. In the midst of all this messiness, there is now no condemnation for those who are in Christ Jesus. In Jesus, we have the message — the Word from God — that we are accepted in our dependency and finitude, that we are loved and accepted in the messiness of the flesh, that we are known and loved in our individuality.

Over the next few weeks, we'll be looking at life in the Spirit, but for now, I want to give a preview of it. Paul emphasizes that in Jesus Christ we are offered a new opportunity in our lives, an opportunity to unlearn some of the ways of the flesh, an opportunity to affirm our neediness and our dependence. It is an opportunity to encounter the true source of our lives, the God we know in Jesus Christ. It is why Jesus emphasizes that if we really want to meet him, we shall go to those in need, especially the poor. That's where we will find Jesus. This is what the New Testament tells us again and again. In order to meet Jesus, don't look to the people who are rich and powerful and famous, look to those who are struggling; not just to help them, but to find life for ourselves. Paul lifts up this opportunity, to encounter this humanity of Jesus: "For God has done what the law, weakened by the flesh, could not do; sending God's own Son in the likeness of sinful flesh, and for sin, he condemned sin in the flesh." John's Gospel put it another way in chapter 1. "The Word became flesh and dwelt among us." John doesn't say the word became human. He says that the Word became flesh. Jesus came into all the prejudices of his culture and said "No" to the flight from God. He learned from someone that women were less than men, but he said "No" to that teaching. He learned from somebody that Gentiles were not like him, but he said, "No."

The life of Jesus offers us the opportunity to see this journey, to see someone who knows these struggles and who wrestles with them. This is what Paul means when he talks about the humanity of Jesus, that Jesus has entered into the struggles of our existence, into this process of the flesh. As the hymn puts it, "Jesus knows our every weakness." because he has struggled in the process of what it means to be human in the flesh. Jesus shows us a different way of responding to our dependency and our individuality, turning toward God rather than turning toward the idols of the world. It is what Paul calls "Spirit."

By Spirit, Paul does not mean flight from the world or flight from human existence. Paul's point is not to get us out of the world but rather to get us *into* the world as children of God, as authentic human beings. When anxiety strikes us, as it almost surely will and does almost daily, Paul tells us to refrain from fleeing from our anxiety by running to the idols. Rather, turn to the Spirit. Paul urges us to cry out "Abba," "Daddy," and to ask God to preserve us and to give us life. We will be exploring this theme of Spirit more in the weeks ahead, but for today, let us hear that Paul urges us to hear the good news of the life, death, and resurrection of Jesus Christ. It's not just something that happened way back in the past. It's something that is happening this very moment in our lives, as we struggle with what it means to be a human being.

Jesus knows our finitude and our individuality and our anxiety. He knows the ways of the flesh. Yet he shows us a different way to respond, a way that we are asked to hear in his life, death, and resurrection — the way of the Spirit. We are asked to hear some unbelievable and stunning news. The source of all of life and the source of our life — God — desires us, loves us, and wants us. God knows all of our idolatry, all the parts of our being, and God wants to free us from our captivity. God loves us, God knows us, and God wants us. God calls us out to hear, to receive, and to believe the good news. This is the good news by which we are saved. This is the good news by which we have life. This is the life of the Spirit. Amen.

Staying In This World
Romans 8:18-30
November 8, 1998

I could preach on this text for a month of Sundays and never exhaust its richness or its meaning. It has so many verses and sayings that are familiar to us. Verse 18 talks about perseverance in suffering. "I consider that the sufferings of this present time are not worth comparing with the glory about to be revealed to us."

Verse 19 emphasizes the anticipation that is ours in Christ Jesus. "For the creation waits with eager longing for the revealing of the children of God." Verse 21 lifts up the freedom that is God's gift to us. "That the creation itself will be set free from its bondage to decay and will obtain the freedom of the glory of the children of God." Then, two verses which speak to us of the struggles in our hearts and in our lives, verses 26 and 28. "Likewise the Spirit helps us in our weakness; for we do not know how to pray as we ought, but that very Spirit intercedes with sighs too deep for words." "We know that all things work together for good for those who love God."

Any of these verses are worth a sermon by themselves, and we have not even spoken of the important theological doctrines rooted in these verses: predestination, adoption, and providence. We could go many places for a sermon on this text, but today I want to focus on Paul's doctrine of the Spirit in these verses. Chapter 8 of Romans begins with a contrast between flesh and Spirit.

> *For those who live according to the flesh set their minds on the things of the flesh, but those who live according to the Spirit set their minds on the things of the Spirit. To set the mind on the flesh is death, but to set the mind on the Spirit is life and peace.*
> — Romans 8:5-6

Earlier in this series on Romans, we looked at Paul's concept of flesh, and I want to take a few moments to review that. Flesh is

71

our idolatrous response as human beings to our being finite and mortal, to our discovery that we are separate individuals, that we have an individual consciousness. We answer the anxiety raised by our finitude and our individuality by choosing the idols of the world. Flesh is not the body or sexuality, as the church so often emphasizes. Paul's idea of "flesh" is much deeper and broader than that. It is the process by which we learn to use the idols of the world to answer and assuage our anxieties. This process doesn't drop out of the sky onto us, and we aren't born with it. *We learn it.*

Paul emphasizes this struggle and this process and uses a feminine image to describe it.

> *We know that the whole creation has been groaning in labor pains until now; and not only the creation, but we ourselves, who have the first fruits of the Spirit, groan inwardly while we wait for adoption, the redemption of our bodies.* — Romans 8:22-23

Earlier, he described it as being in bondage to decay. We groan in our struggles to be real and to know that we are loved. We learn from those we trust that the idols of the world — idols like sexism — will help us and ease our fears. Yet, the idols only lead us to further alienation from God, from one another, and from ourselves. This is the process that Paul is describing when he uses the term "flesh."

Are we lost without hope, groaning and groping in our bondage to decay? No. Paul offers us the other side, the doctrine of Spirit is the power that Paul affirms as our source of life and hope. Spirit has many manifestations, but we should note that the essence of Spirit is God working in our lives, calling to us, seeking us out, wanting us to know that we are desired and loved, letting us know that we are known. Spirit is not another semi-god, not an angelic messenger from God. Spirit is God, longing for us to see and to experience a new reality and to begin to live in that new reality. In this passage in Romans Paul lifts up several characteristics of life in the Spirit, of life redefined, of ourselves redefined, of life in this new reality.

The first characteristic is *reorientation*. Paul urges us to hear that it is possible to be reoriented toward a different way of life in the midst of our lives that are caught up in the complex web of idolatrous definitions. Paul wants us to hear that God has come among us in Jesus Christ to set us free. Paul urges us to hear and to see and to believe that there is a whole different way of perceiving ourselves and of perceiving reality. Paul emphasizes that God has come among us in Jesus Christ to help us understand who we are and who God is.

This is what Jesus meant in the first chapter of Mark's Gospel when Jesus seems to literally burst upon the scene, proclaiming the arrival of the reign of God. "The time is fulfilled, and the kingdom of God has come near; repent, and believe in the good news." I grew up believing that "repent" meant to stop doing bad things, a belief that is reflective of many teachings in the church. It is a belief that emphasizes the power and the necessity of the will. The Greek word that underlies "repent" certainly means to change our behavior, but it also means something deeper and more difficult. It means to turn around, to reorient our lives. It means to change not only our will but also our attitude, to change the way we perceive reality. When we are asked to repent, we are asked to change our view of the nature of things, to take a look and to see a different level of reality.

Jesus and Paul urge this shift not because we are so bad, but because we have such limited imaginations. Our identities and our lives are so intertwined with the idols of the world that we cannot even imagine life without their categories, much less seek to live a different life. This is the real power of the flesh, that our imaginations became so truncated that we cannot behold the vision of the reign of God. Our actions that hurt us, hurt others, and hurt God grow not so much out of a weak will as out of a limited imagination. In chapter 8 of Romans, Paul urges us to hear about the power of the Spirit. He urges us to undergo a reorientation toward ourselves and toward others. Paul urges us to hear the good news, that in the life, death, and resurrection of Jesus Christ we have the opportunity to see that God loves us and wants us, that God knows us, all of us, all of our hopes and longings, all of our failures and idolatry. Paul urges us to believe in the enduring reality of the power of God. Life in the Spirit, then, is characterized first of all by a reorientation of our lives toward God.

Life in the Spirit is also characterized by freedom. Paul emphasizes this strongly in the beginning of chapter 5 of Galatians. "For freedom Christ has set us free. Stand firm, therefore, and do not submit again to a yoke of slavery." Here in Romans, Paul puts it another way; we "will obtain the freedom of the glory of the children of God." By "freedom" Paul is not using the modern idea of a lack of constraints. He is not using "freedom" as so many talk show hosts use it in our day, where there is no engagement, no one to bother us, where we are disconnected from everyone, where there are no limits. Freedom, for Paul, means possibilities to move against our fate, that we are not totally anchored and bound to the categories of the world, which we have learned and accepted. Freedom means room to move in our consciousness, room for us to move, room for God to move. "Freedom" for Paul means that we are not totally tied down to the idols of the world, that there is room for God to move in our being. Paul means that because of Jesus Christ, we can imagine the world and ourselves differently, that we can imagine God, that we can imagine a different life.

We do this not by *repressing* our passion, as the church so often emphasizes, but rather by *reorienting* and *expressing* our passion. Paul stuns us by indicating that God wants our passion, not our perfection. We cannot deliver perfection anyway, and we delude ourselves if we believe that we can. Paul's language in this text is language full of passion. "Creation waits with eager longing ... for the glorious freedom of the children of God ... groaning in labor pains ... groaning inwardly ... with sighs too deep for words." Paul emphasizes that the freeing power of the Spirit allows us to refocus our passion, from the categories and definitions of the world to God and God's definitions of who we are. He lifts up that in life in the Spirit, we are never confined to the world's definition of ourselves or even to our definition of ourselves, but rather there is always available to us God's definition of ourselves.

A third characteristic of life in the Spirit is that we are called to stay in this life. Often the church insists that its members must flee from this world and escape from the messiness and confusion of life. Paul emphasizes that we are called to stay in the world, to stay in the messiness, though we are not defined by it. The goal of life in the Spirit is not to get us out of this world so that we can be pure. The goal of life in the Spirit is to engage our passion so that we can be in the world in an authentic way, driven not by the idols of the world, but led by the Spirit to affirm and to proclaim that God is at the center of our lives and all of life. Paul is not asking us to escape from the struggles of the world. That is not possible. We may seek to escape them by repressing them in our consciousness or in our institutional life, but in so doing, we only drive them underground and give them much more power by limiting access to them. Rather, Paul is asking us to go back into our struggles and into the struggles of the world, returning with a renewed sense of God's love for us and for the world, with a renewed sense of possibility and hope.

Because we are asked to stay in the world and in our own journeys, Paul emphasizes that life in the Spirit will also be characterized by struggle. He uses images of struggle often in this text, as we have seen. Life in the Spirit is not always sweetness and light. It also involves struggle because the power of the idols is so deeply rooted in our view of ourselves and in our view of the world. Most of us cannot even imagine life without the power of affluence and materialism, and as we begin to wrestle with the hold that money has on our hearts and on our imaginations, it seems like a bottomless pit. We are asked, however, in life in the Spirit to wrestle with this power and begin to hear a new and vital definition of ourselves. It is in these kinds of struggles, where we come to realize how much power materialism, racism, sexism, homophobia, and other idols have in our lives; that we can come to know this characteristic of life in the Spirit. It is here that we know what Paul means when he says that "we groan inwardly while we wait for adoption." We know that groaning in our own journeys.

Paul emphasizes in the passage that God also knows our struggles and our groaning, and that God is working in our lives. He speaks of the Spirit interceding in our prayers, in our longings, in our fears, in our hopes, in those places where the demons are so powerful and scary and interwoven with our own identity that we cannot even articulate them. In Presbyterian worship we often have a time of confession, usually including a time of silent, individual confession. This silent time is pointedly brief, rarely exceeding thirty seconds. Part of the reason it is brief is that our entire worship must be over in an hour or less. Yet a more important reason for the brevity is that we don't want to allow too much time for the powers of the idols to reach our consciousness. We prefer a brief time to consider a few sins and then move on, thereby preventing ourselves from discovering how captive we are to the powers of the world. Paul stresses that it is precisely in these places that the Spirit is moving, moving in us with sighs too deep for words.

Paul also lifts up that famous verse, "We know that all things work together for good for those who love God, who are called according to his purpose." In saying this, Paul does not mean that everything that happens to us is God's will. Paul is well aware of the power of evil, and he is well aware that God has given us freedom, freedom even to make choices that will have disastrous consequences for ourselves and for others. Rather, Paul is saying that God will not abandon us to the idolatrous powers or to the disastrous consequences or to our resultant suffering. In all these, indeed especially in these, God is working with us and in us so that we may know grace, truth, and life; so that we may know to whom we belong.

Paul urges us to move into life in the Spirit, to hear and to receive the good news, to reorient ourselves toward the new reality of Jesus Christ, to hear that God is in our midst, to hear that God wants us and desires us, to hear that God loves us. It is in these places, in life in the Spirit, that our imaginations will be expanded to experience the glorious freedom of the children of God. No one put this concept of life in the Spirit better than did the author of Psalm 139:

> *Lord, you examine me and know me, you know if I am*
> *standing or sitting, you read my thoughts from far away,*
> *whether I walk or lie down, you are watching, you know*
> *every detail of my conduct.*

76

The word is not even on my tongue, Lord, before you know all about it; close behind and close in front you fence me round, shielding me with your hand. Such knowledge is beyond my understanding, a height to which my mind cannot attain.

Where could I go to escape your spirit? Where could I flee from your presence? If I climb the heavens, you are there, there too, if I lie in Sheol.

If I flew to the point of sunrise, or westward across the sea, your hand would still be guiding me, your right hand holding me.

If I asked darkness to cover me, and light to become night around me, that darkness would not be dark to you, night would be as light as day.

It was you who created my inmost self, and put me together in my mother's womb; for all these mysteries I thank you: for the wonder of myself, for the wonder of your works.[1]

For all these mysteries, for the wonder of ourselves, as confused as we are, and for the grace that is bestowed upon us, we say "Thank you." That is the beginning of life in the Spirit. Amen.

---

1. Translation from The Jerusalem Bible, as found in *The Worship Book* (Philadelphia: Westminster Press, 1970), p. 74.

Breaking Down The Barriers

Every year during Black History Month, Stroupe gives a series of sermons on the struggle of African-Americans for justice and equality from the days of slavery through the Civil Rights Movement. While these sermons tell the stories of particular lives that have burned brightly as witnesses for justice in this struggle, many of the lives lifted up are often unfamiliar to many at Oakhurst, and to Americans in general, white or black. As an integrated congregation, Oakhurst's own story has been significantly marked by both the story of race in America and the biblical story. Consequently, these sermons are central to the life of Oakhurst in its attempt to be the church and live out the Good News of Jesus Christ in a context (both local and national) still defined by racism. Because Stroupe understands the proclamation of the Good News of Jesus Christ to necessarily entail the struggle for justice and racial equality, he presents lives and voices from that struggle as the "great cloud of witnesses" calling us to follow them along the difficult path of faithfulness to the gospel.

Keep Your Lamps Trimmed And Burnin'
Luke 5:33-39; Matthew 25:1-13
February 6, 2000

She was born into slavery 100 miles south of the Mason-Dixon Line. The principalities and powers were structured so that she would be taught to believe that being a slave was her natural calling. The power of slavery tried to pound its definition into her. "You are a slave. You're supposed to be a slave." She did not know what year she was born. She never learned to read or write. She was sold away from her family when she was six years old, and her new mistress beat her so badly that the scars were with her forever. When she was a teenager, her master hit her in the head with a heavy object, and she suffered permanent brain damage.

Slavery tried to beat her down physically and spiritually, but she refused to yield to its definition of her. She heard a voice that was different from the voice of slavery. She heard that her primary definition was not "slave." She heard that her primary definition was what our choirs sing of being, "a child of God." She heard that she was a slave, not because of who she was, but because of who white people were. Hearing the voice of Jesus, hearing this new definition was like receiving new wine, giving her hope and life, and that gave her the determination to be free. She first tried to run away from slavery when she was eight years old, but she was captured and was severely beaten for it. Finally, in 1849, she escaped permanently at about age eighteen, and she continued to fight against slavery for the rest of her life. Indeed, by the time of the Civil War in 1861, there were two ex-slaves who stood head and shoulders above all the rest in their efforts to combat slavery. One was Frederick Douglass, the giant of the nineteenth century. The other was born Araminta Ross, born about 1821 on Maryland's eastern shore, near where Frederick Douglass grew up as a slave. Araminta Ross was known as "Minty" in her childhood years, but as a teenager, she took her momma's name, Harriet. After she got married, her name became so famous that by 1868, a biography of her life had already been written by Sarah Bradford. Today, in our county library, there are 57 books about her. The name by which she became famous is Harriet Tubman, and we will look at her story today.

"Keep your lamps trimmed and burnin', keep your lamps trimmed and burnin', keep your lamps trimmed and burnin', get ready for the judgment day." This song is based on a parable of Jesus in Matthew 25, and it was a theme song of Harriet Tubman's, along with "Go Down Moses." It touched her because it reminded her and other people held as slaves of the importance of refusing to allow the definition of slavery to take over their spirits. It spoke of a new definition, of new wine, of the in-breaking power of God. This new wine was particularly powerful for Harriet Tubman because, after she escaped slavery in 1849, she was not content to stay in the relative safety of the North. She came back south again and again to lead others into freedom. She made nineteen trips, leading over 300 people to freedom from slavery. She became known as "Moses" along the Underground Railroad.

Her whole life was a witness against the powers of oppression, whether it was slavery before the Civil War or whether it was working for women's rights after the Civil War, fighting against male dominance. She was always an advocate for poor people. She had been thinking about escaping from slavery most of her life. She hesitated, though, because most of her family, including her husband, did not want to try it. She could not read or write, and she had no idea how to escape from slavery, but she dreamed about it.

> I seemed to see a line, and on the other side of the line were green fields, and lovely flowers, and beautiful white ladies, who stretched out their arms to me over the line, but I couldn't reach them. I always fell before I got to the line.[1]

Rumors in the slave network gave her two clues about escaping. One was the North Star; you followed the North Star in the constellation known as the Drinking Gourd. I grew up calling that constellation the Big Dipper, but in Harriet Tubman's network it was the Drinking Gourd, and it was said that nearby there was a white woman who was against slavery and who was known to help people who wanted to flee from slavery. In 1849, Harriet's master died, and it was said in the slave cabins that the master's son was going to sell Harriet and some of her brothers in order to pay off the father's debts. Harriet Tubman decided that it was time to escape from slavery before she was sold off into the Deep South. She tried to convince her husband to go with her, but he said, "No." She finally talked her three brothers into going with her. They fled into the woods at night, but her three brothers got scared and went back, leaving her alone.

She headed for the white woman's house that she had heard about, and there she did find an ally. That woman gave her money and directions to the next safe house. When Harriet Tubman knocked on the door of the next house, a white woman greeted her abruptly and harshly, calling her names and making her sweep the porch. Harriet was despondent. She thought she had gone to the wrong house and would be returned to slavery. But later on, the same woman brought her into the house and apologized to her for the harsh treatment. The woman was certain that slave-catchers were watching the house, and so she had to be deceptive. There, in that house, Harriet Tubman learned the necessity of trickery and deception in this business of flight to freedom. She heard the story of the midwives of Israel in the book of Exodus who deceived Pharaoh and lied to him in order to save the Hebrew babies. She learned this from a white woman on the Underground Railroad.

Harriet Tubman was passed from house to house and finally crossed into Pennsylvania, where there was no slavery. These are some of her memories of that crossing.

> *When I found I had crossed that line, I looked at my hands to see if I was the same person. There was such glory over everything; the sun came like gold through the trees, and over the fields, and I felt like I was in Heaven.* [2]

She eventually made it to Philadelphia and did domestic work there, earning money for a change. She saved her money to finance trips back south and bring her other family members out of slavery. In Philadelphia, she also met William Still, an African-American who was a leader in the Underground Railroad. She learned from him about a whole network of black folk and white folk, many of them in the Society of Friends (derisively known as "Quakers"), who were helping people escape from slavery. Through Still, she met Thomas Garrett, a white man in Wilmington who financed many of her trips south.

In 1850, she returned twice to Maryland to bring some of her family members out. In 1851, she went to get her husband but found that he had remarried and did not want to go. It hurt her heart. She also felt another sting during this time period. On September 18, 1850, Congress passed its second Fugitive Slave Act. The first one had been passed in 1793 and had stripped people escaping slavery of the right to trial by jury. It gave power to federal judges to hear cases of people escaping from slavery and to decide their fate. Because it seemed to violate the Constitution, many northern states refused to enforce it. In 1850, the Southern bloc in Congress got a second act passed that was much harsher than the first. It set up special commissioners throughout the North to hear the pleas of slave owners who wanted to reclaim their "escaped property." A fee was to be paid to the commissioner, and if the commissioner returned the person to the slave owner, the fee was doubled, and with this financial incentive, slaves began to be sent back. The second Fugitive Slave Act also made it a federal crime for anyone to assist those people escaping slavery. This Act caused a firestorm in the 1850s and was one of the things that led to the Civil War.

Harriet Tubman decided at this point to take her people to Canada and not to leave them in the United States. She became legendary on the Underground Railroad. Oh, yes, the slave owners heard about her, too, and they offered rewards totaling $52,000 for her capture, dead or alive. She was never captured, however, for she was a master of discipline, disguise, and deception. She carried a gun with her at all times. She carried a gun to combat the masters. She often said that she would never be taken alive. But, she also carried a gun to combat the fears of those escaping slavery. Occasionally, those escaping from slavery panicked and wanted to turn back. When they asked Harriet Tubman for permission to go back, she gave them a choice. They could either continue to go with her, or they could die right there. She was not going to let them go back. She had two reasons for her harsh stance. First, she wanted them to hear that new definition of themselves, that they were children of God, not slaves. She wanted them to hear it not just when things were going well, but in difficult times, when tough choices had to be made. Second, she knew that if they went back, they would be tortured until they told the secrets of the Underground Railroad, and she wanted to protect those secrets.

She had not communicated with her parents because she feared that they would be tortured, also. Finally, in the spring of 1857, she went back to Maryland to bring them out of slavery. They were too old to walk, and so she took a bold course. She disguised herself as an old black woman driving a load of hay in a wagon. Underneath that hay were her parents. She drove for miles and took them into freedom in Pennsylvania. She made her last trip for freedom in December, 1860, bringing seven people out of slavery. It was not her last trip South, however. She came to South Carolina early in the Civil War as a nurse and a spy for the Union. After the Civil War, she continued her work for justice. She fought for her people's rights as they were stripped away again and again. She fought for women's rights and for rights for poor people. The money that she made from her 1868 biography was used to start a home for aging black people without money. Though she never learned to read, though she bore the scars of slavery in her heart and on her body, and though she had permanent brain damage from slavery, she was a giant, a fighter for freedom. She had drunk the new wine and had found vision and hope and endurance.

"Keep your lamps trimmed and burnin'." That was the anthem for Harriet Tubman. Get ready for the in-breaking of God! Slavery sought to define and oppress and defeat Harriet Tubman. It was a powerful system, and it had the power to cripple the spirit and the body. It was a difficult power to overcome because it chained not just the body. It sought to chain the spirit of the people held as slaves. It was not only the masters "out there" that sought to define Harriet Tubman as a slave. It also sought to make her believe in her own heart, "in here," that she should be a slave.

Masters and slaves alike were crippled by slavery. Slaves, of course, suffered the brunt of the oppression. Yet, we must not lose sight of the cost of slavery and racism to the humanity of the white masters. We lost our humanity in slavery. As difficult and as powerful as slavery was, the truth remains that its central power came from getting people to say, "Yes" to it, from the masters saying, "Yes," and from the slaves saying, "Yes." Masters believed that it was their right and their duty to crush the humanity of other people, and slaves began believing that it was their own fault that they were being crushed.

Harriet Tubman, like many others held as slaves, refused to believe those definitions. She had drunk from that new wine. She was a child of God, and no one was going to take that definition from her. She took in that new wine that Jesus talked about. She believed that the new reality of God was breaking into her life. The definition of herself that she received from God did not fit slavery's definition of who she was. Those definitions clashed, just as Jesus indicated that they would when he spoke about the new wine not fitting into the old wineskins.

We must take special note that Harriet Tubman had many limitations. She was not an eloquent speaker, no Sojourner Truth here. She could not read or write, no Frederick Douglass here. She was sickly all her life, often going into trances or falling unconscious. Yet she was fired up by that new wine, by that vision of a new reality. She was not a slave by definition. She was enslaved by the principalities and powers, but she struggled for freedom. It was costly and painful, but her heart was set free after tasting that new wine. She would never be the same. She would keep her lamps trimmed and burnin'. She burned for freedom.

May it be so with us. In the midst of all the principalities and powers, in the midst of all the demonic definitions that have come into our lives and have taken root in our hearts, may we taste that new wine. We have allowed many definitions to capture our hearts and imaginations, whether it's money or skin color or gender or sexual orientation or nationality or any of a host of others. In the midst of these definitions, may we, too, taste that new wine in our lives. May we, too, glimpse and grasp that new reality that is breaking into our lives to tell us that we are children of God. May we, too, live out of that new reality. May we, too, keep our lamps trimmed and burnin'. Amen.

---

1. Megan McClard, *Harriet Tubman: Slavery and the Underground Railroad* (Englewood Cliffs, New Jersey: Silver Burdett Press, 1991), p. 52.

2. *Ibid.*, p. 62

And A Little Child Shall Lead Them
1 Timothy 4:11-16; 2 Timothy 1:2-7
February 18, 1996

It has been called the most stubborn county in the United States. It is Prince Edward County in the state of Virginia, with the small town of Farmville as its center. Prince Edward County is at the northern end of the great Black Belt that runs through the South. It cuts across the Carolinas to Georgia, through Alabama and Mississippi to the Mississippi River and beyond, for a thousand miles. Because of its rich soil and large black population, it has had a profound effect on the history of the South and of the nation. Prince Edward County is at the northern part of that great southwestern curve. Though it is a small, farming county, in the 1950s it would become a focal point of one of the central themes in American history: race vs. equality. It is a theme and a struggle that is at the heart of our nation. It began when the first African people were brought to these shores in chains. It is a theme and a struggle that continues this very morning. For hundreds of years, it has been at the center of our collective lives.

The state of Virginia, in many ways, has been a remarkable state in our nation's history. By 1800, it was the most populous state and the most influential in the country. It has been called the birthplace of democracy in this country, giving rise to Thomas Jefferson and George Washington and to six other presidents of the United States. Yet, fifty years later, just prior to the Civil War, its star had fallen. In 1845, its percentage of white people attending public schools was among the lowest in the nation. The state of Massachusetts, with about the same population, had fifteen times as many children attending public schools as did Virginia. For all of its legacy of democracy, Virginia has been a state dominated by aristocracy. In 1940, only fifty years ago, just ten out of every one hundred Virginians were eligible to vote. It was a state that fought to keep things the way they were in 1800, with only an elite few in control. Most people, black and white, were controlled by this elite, with race used as a wedge to keep people apart, to keep people from getting together and changing things.

It should be no surprise, then, that the state of Virginia led the "massive resistance" movement in the South, resistance to the 1954 Supreme Court decision of *Brown v. Board of Education*. Orval Faubus of Arkansas, Ross Barnett in Mississippi, and George Wallace in Alabama were all governors who sought to block black entrance into segregated public education in their states, but they eventually yielded to federal power. The state of Virginia closed its public schools rather than integrate them. It closed its public schools rather than allowing black children to go to school with white children. This move, of course, closed public education to both white and black children. Into this glare of stubborn resistance to equality came Prince Edward County. After Virginia had been forced to re-open its public schools, Prince Edward County held out for four more years. It would be the last county in Virginia to re-open its public schools.

For all of its contrariness, and indeed because of its contrariness, Prince Edward County has produced some remarkable citizens. One was Robert Moton, who was right-hand man to Booker T. Washington and was Washington's successor at Tuskegee Institute. Another was Vernon Johns, one of the big three of black preaching at the middle of this century. A third was Barbara Rose Johns, at whom we will look today. She was the oldest child of Robert and Violet Johns, and she was the niece of Vernon Johns.

She was born in New York City in 1935 and died in Philadelphia in 1991. Several years after her birth in New York, her parents gave up on finding steady work in New York because of the Depression. They moved back to her mother's family farm in Prince Edward County, one of the few black families to own land in that county. The family got the money when her maternal grandmother's husband had been killed in an accident in North Carolina, and with the small amount of money they received, they bought land. When Barbara Johns' family moved back to Prince Edward County they moved in with her maternal grandmother, whose name was Mary Croner. From her maternal grandmother, Barbara Johns learned about an unshakable love in her life, the love of God. She was told over and over by her grandmother, Mary Croner, that God's love was enduring and strong. No matter what white people told her, she must remember that there was a love that would not let her go. A love that would define her as a child of God. She learned love from her maternal grandmother.

She also learned at the feet of her paternal grandmother Sally Johns, mother of Robert and Vernon Johns. At this woman's feet, Barbara Johns learned about justice and courage. She would later say about her grandmother Sally Johns, "She had no fear, and she was not the slightest bit subservient to whites."[1] From Mary Croner, Barbara Johns learned about the enduring power of love. From Sally Johns, she learned about the enduring call to justice. She would need both of these as she encountered the principalities and powers in Prince Edward County, Virginia.

Prince Edward County did not build a black high school until 1939. They named it after Robert Moton. It was woefully inadequate from the start, little more than a huge tarpaper shack. It had no gym, no cafeteria, no auditorium, and terrible heating. Youth would take turns standing by the heater to get warm, then go put on their coats at the other end of the room. Despite all this, the black students came to school. By 1947, the number of students was more than twice what the school could accommodate, and there was an obvious crisis. Black parents began to petition the school board, which was all white, to obey the "separate but equal" clause of the 1896 *Plessy v. Ferguson* Supreme Court decision. "Build us a decent high school," they demanded, but the board of education's response was the same as it always had been and always would be, "No money."

Three black men were leaders in the fight for a new black high school. One was the Reverend Francis Griffin, pastor of First Baptist Church in Farmville. He was a courageous man and had been part of the first Negro unit in General George S. Patton's tank corps in Europe. His boyhood friend, John Lancaster, now the Negro county agricultural agent, joined him in this campaign for a new school. The third was Boyd Jones, who was principal at Moton High School. Keeping all of these black men in check was the white superintendent of the schools, T. J. McIlwane. Born in

Japan to Presbyterian missionaries, he did not believe that black people could learn as well as white people. He sought to keep the system in check in order to reflect his belief, and he held it in check until Barbara Johns answered God's call.

Barbara Johns chafed under the conditions at Moton High. She thought about it during the summer of 1950, between her sophomore and junior years in high school. She felt that her generation must do something, must act. She loved her parents and their generation, and she knew that they were good people. But she felt that her parents' generation had lost its boldness because they had lived too long under the racist system. She felt that they had come to accept the white view, that nothing could or would change. She continued to be distressed as she began her junior year in high school in the fall of 1950. She was sixteen years old.

She talked with her teachers about the situation of not having an adequate school. One day one of her teachers challenged her. "Why don't you do something about it?" The teacher's challenge stung her, but it also inspired her. A few days later, she asked Connie Stokes, who was president of the student council at Moton High, and Connie's brother John, a top student and athlete, to meet with her. They met out on the field, away from everyone else. As John Stokes remembered it, she spoke with great effectiveness. "She opened our eyes to a lot of things. She emphasized that we must follow our parents, but in some instances — and I remember her saying this very vividly — a little child shall lead them."[2]

Connie and John Stokes agreed to join with Barbara Johns in planning an action, and they recruited two more students to begin the planning. They would monitor the situation to see what the school board would do, and they would each bring one more trusted student into the circle. No adults, though. No teachers, either, and especially not Principal Boyd Jones, whom they admired, but who, they knew, would be obligated to squelch their action. What was the action that they were planning? To go on strike, to boycott classes until the white school board agreed to build a new black high school.

By late April, 1951, the white school board had made no moves toward building a new black high school. Over the weekend of April 21, the word was passed among the inner circle of students:

take action on Monday. Shortly before eleven in the morning on Monday, April 23, 1951, Principal Boyd Jones got an urgent phone call at his office, telling him that two of his students were at the Farmville bus station. He was told that the police were hassling the students and that they would surely get in trouble if he did not immediately come to the bus station. He left hurriedly, and the students went into action. They had made that phone call to Boyd Jones. Student monitors took notes to the teachers, calling for an assembly at eleven o'clock, the usual hour for such assemblies. Barbara Johns had signed the notes the way the principal usually did, with the letter "J."

The students and the teachers gathered in the makeshift assembly room, and when the curtains were pulled back, they were astonished to see young Barbara Johns at the podium, with the strike committee seated behind her. Barbara Johns called for order, then she invited the teachers to leave. The teachers had no idea what was going on. What they saw was a dangerous, unauthorized situation. Some teachers moved forward to take over the assembly, but on signal from Barbara Johns, a group of student marshals stood up to block the way. Barbara Johns took off her shoe and rapped it sharply on the podium, and she said, "I want all of the teachers out of here."[3] And most of them left. Principal Boyd Jones got back from the bus station and came into the meeting, but to his credit, he did not intervene.

Barbara Johns then spoke eloquently from her heart. It was time that they were treated equally with white people. It was time for them to have a decent high school building. It was time for the students to take leadership in making this possible. Then she made the proposal. They were going to march out of school then and there, and they were going to stay out until the white community agreed to build a new black high school. The boycott was on and it held, despite great stress. Barbara Johns got home that night, and she told her grandmother, Mary Croner, "Grandma, I walked out of school today, and I carried 450 students with me." "It took my breath away," her grandmother later recalled. "You reckon you done the right thing?" she asked. "I believe so," Barbara answered, and added, "Stick with us."[4]

The strike was supported by the three black men that I named earlier in the sermon. The Reverend Francis Griffin opened his church. Rather than going to school each day, the students went to First Baptist Church. Reverend Griffin also helped them write a letter to lawyers at the NAACP, asking for their help. On Wednesday, April 25, attorneys Oliver Hill and Spottswood Robinson arrived from Richmond, representing the NAACP. They were impressed with the student initiative and action, but they told them that the NAACP would not support the demand for a black high school. What they would support, however, was a demand for desegregation. One high school. One student body.

The lawyers were skeptical about the adult support since this was a student-led movement. They were skeptical about what the students could accomplish since few adults were in leadership. They promised to return the next night if the students could deliver adults at the meeting. The call went out among the black community. The next night, 1,000 black people gathered at Moton High School to hear the plan. It was debated, fiercely. Should we take the step and ask for desegregation? It was voted and agreed to accept the NAACP proposal to enter a lawsuit for desegregation rather than to seek a new black high school. The lawsuit was filed, and a fourteen-year-old girl, Dorothy Davis, was the first person listed on the suit. It became known as *Davis v. Prince Edward County.*

The NAACP lawyers filed suit in the United States District Court of Virginia, and the case was heard late in February, 1952, in Richmond. One week later, the court returned a unanimous verdict against the black students of Prince Edward County, saying that education was a states' rights issue and that only the states should decide it. On July 12, 1952, the NAACP filed an appeal of the *Davis* decision with the United States Supreme Court. The Supreme Court agreed to hear it, but it was also joined with four other similar cases, making one big case. At this juncture the white school board in Prince Edward County agreed to build a new black high school. They had somehow found the funds.

But the die was cast. On December 9, 1952, opening arguments began before the United States Supreme Court on these five cases. Fifty-six years after *Plessy v. Ferguson*, 87 years after the abolition of slavery in the Thirteenth Amendment, 163 years after the ratification of the United States Constitution, and 333 years after the first African people were brought in chains to the shores of this country, the highest court in the land convened to hear arguments about whether white people could continue to treat black people as property and as slaves. The case was called *Brown v. Board of Education of Topeka, Kansas.* Thurgood Marshall would be the lead attorney for the NAACP, but a little child had led them to that place. A sixteen-year-old nurtured by the love of one grandmother. A sixteen-year-old fired by the vision of justice from her other grandmother. A sixteen-year-old, named Barbara Johns, had followed the advice the Apostle Paul had given his young protégé Timothy. "Set an example for all the believers. Do not neglect the gift that has been given to you."

We give thanks for Barbara Johns and many other witnesses like her. She did not neglect the gift that had been given to her. She set an example for all of us who are believers. We give thanks for her and for all those who surrounded her and nurtured her. We give thanks that she witnessed to the truth that we belong to one another. We need her story and her witness today, because we are still not sure if we accept that 8-0 decision that came from the Supreme Court on May 17, 1954, in the *Brown* case. We're still not sure if we believe that black people and white people belong together. In our struggles, when we long for clarity and courage, let us remember this sixteen-year-old who set an example in the faith. May we step into her circle of witnesses in our time. Amen.

---

1. Richard Kluger, *Simple Justice* (New York: Random House, 1975), p. 454.

2. *Ibid.*, p. 467.

3. Taylor Branch, *Parting The Waters* (New York: Simon and Schuster, 1988, p. 20.

4. *Op. cit.*, Kluger, p. 471. For an expanded version of this story and many others, see Kluger's excellent book, with chapter 19 as the focus.

The River Of Justice
Amos 5:18-24
January 14, 2001

It has taken a long time, but Martin Luther King, Jr., has become an American hero. Today is part of King Weekend, leading up to the national holiday in his name. It was made a holiday in 1983 — almost twenty years ago — when God showed a sense of humor in the fact that President Ronald Reagan was forced to sign the legislation proclaiming a national holiday in honor of Martin Luther King, Jr. Today, Dr. King has almost been made a saint. The Roman Catholic Church has nominated him as a martyr. Coca-Cola celebrates him, and now the Atlanta Symphony plays in his honor. He was one of the great orators in our nation's history. His "I Have A Dream" speech in August, 1963, is among the best in American history.

Martin Luther King, Jr., was special. For thirteen years he was the focal point of an amazing non-violent revolution in our country, a revolution in which we as a nation were compelled to reaffirm the true meaning of our calling as a people. "We hold these truths to be self-evident, that all people are created equal." Dr. King understood this calling as a driving force in American history, this idea of having equal dignity as a child of God. He captured it well in his famous 1963 speech.

> So I say to you, my friends, that even though we must face the difficulties of today and tomorrow, I still have a dream. It is a dream deeply rooted in the American dream that one day this nation will rise up and live out the true meaning of its creed — we hold these truths to be self-evident, that all men are created equal.
>
> I have a dream my four little children will one day live in a nation where they will not be judged by the color of their skin but by the content of their character. I have a dream today![1]

When we come together to celebrate King Day we are celebrating his life and the vision that gave him life. But we are also celebrating, remembering, and rededicating ourselves to that vision and to that calling, to that river of women and men and children and youth that has flowed throughout our nation's history, the river of those who have lived, died, struggled, and fought for the idea of equality, who have echoed the call of Amos to his society, "Let justice roll down like water and righteousness like an ever-flowing stream." That ever-flowing stream has sometimes gone underground — indeed, in some eras in our history it has almost dried up. At other times, though, it has flowed with a mighty roar, always calling us to wade in the water to join in the struggle for justice.

In the midst of our remembering and celebrating, we must always recall how much of a menace Martin Luther King, Jr., was, how many times he was arrested for "disturbing the peace." Indeed, he was disturbing the peace — he was challenging things as they were. Martin Luther King, Jr., represented a dangerous vision. He was arrested 29 times. He served time in Georgia's infamous Reidsville prison. His house was bombed, he was stabbed, and he and his family were constantly under death threats. Yes, he was finally assassinated.

Why? Why all this furor for a man who advocated equality? First of all, because he asked white people to come out of denial. I want to share my response to Martin Luther King, Jr., as a white boy who grew up in a delta of the Mississippi River in the 1950s and 1960s. For me, Martin Luther King, Jr., was not a hero — he was the devil. He was a plague, a communist, an outside agitator interfering with the God-given order of life and of my life.

For many of us in that era who were white, he embodied all that was threatening to us — a sense of foreboding about the presence of black people in our midst, and an awareness (unspoken and often not even allowed to come to consciousness) of a basic injustice. He offered a different vision of humanity, not a hierarchy with white people on top but rather a circle, a family of many colors and many languages.

Martin Luther King, Jr., brought that vision — an exceedingly threatening vision to those of us who are white. Many white people, including myself, said, "No." We simply could not abide that vision. Yet his vision and prophecy and example were so powerful that many of us began to reconsider. One of King's great attributes was that he invited white folks into the conversation. He invited me as a Southern white Christian man to reconsider my true identity and my true calling. He invited me and others to reconsider what we thought was the God-given order and routine.

One of his great legacies is that he invited white people to consider our humanity, to reconsider our calling as Americans, as people who were actually part of the family of humanity, not at the top of it, but part of it. For those of us who are Christian, he invited us to reconsider our calling and our definition as disciples of Jesus. This is what made King so exciting — and so dangerous. But, he didn't stop there. He broadened his own vision to connect racism and poverty and materialism and war. The director of the FBI called him the most dangerous man in America because of this connection. On April 4, 1967, he addressed Clergy and Laity Concerned at Riverside Church in New York and announced publicly his opposition to the war being waged in Vietnam. Exactly one year later, to the day, he was assassinated in Memphis.

Martin Luther King, Jr., was a dangerous man because he began to understand our nation's policy of promoting the rich and cursing the poor. As he indicated in his 1967 speech, he began to see a pattern in our foreign policy — to destabilize or to overthrow governments that seem to threaten our wealth. We do have — and continue to have — a long, sordid history of this sort of behavior with regard to the rest of the world; from Chile to Guatemala to Iran and many others. The Reagan administration obliterated a generation in Nicaragua in order to fight communism, a smokescreen that sought to cover our real motive: "Don't mess with our money." Our proclaimed creed is to promote democracy, but as we saw in the recent presidential election, we don't even trust democracy in our own country, much less in other countries.[2] We will soon be inaugurating a president who understands the *real* creed of the United States: "Make the world safe for capitalism."[3]

97

He is assembling a cabinet who well understands that real creed, even using African-Americans like Colin Powell and Condoleezza Rice.

Though the Republicans express it most openly, it's not just Republicans who profess this creed. After all, it was Democratic President Bill Clinton who allied himself with Newt Gingrich and the rich to push through NAFTA, the Free Trade Act that seeks to make the world safe for capitalism. It is this creed that Martin Luther King, Jr., began to question. It was this creed that King began to understand. He began to see how much it clashed with the ideas of justice and equality. He began to question the American creed that money and materialism are the answers to the problems of justice and equality.

Dr. King became dangerous in America when he began to make these connections, when he began to connect racism and materialism and militarism. We must remember that he was killed in Memphis not over a voting rights issue but over a paycheck issue. He had gone to Memphis to help garbage workers form a union. We must also remember that when he was killed, he was in the middle of organizing The Poor Peoples' Campaign, beginning with a march on Washington to demand justice for the poor. Martin Luther King, Jr., was a menace to mainstream America because he began to understand that racism and economics are vitally connected, because he began to understand that the God movement is about justice for the poor, not about individual salvation, not about getting black people on the board of Coca-Cola or selecting Colin Powell as Secretary of State. This vision of justice for the poor is dangerous — it got Jesus killed, and it got Martin Luther King, Jr., killed.

This weekend of celebration, then, is not just a time for remembering a great preacher and leader. It is also a time to look at ourselves and ask ourselves a decisive question: Which stream will we follow? The mainstream of American life, which sees materialism as the answer, or this ever-flowing stream that calls for justice to roll down like waters? The witness and the legacy of Martin Luther King, Jr., asks us to consider our calling and to decide where to wade in the waters.

98

We are worshiping today on ground once occupied by Native Americans. Indeed, the crossroads at the Decatur Square once marked the boundary between Creek and Cherokee tribes, the Creek to the South and the Cherokee to the North. In our Advent study last year on Appalachia, we learned about the Trail of Tears, about the Cherokee people being forcibly removed from North Georgia by Democratic President Andrew Jackson. They were removed because gold had been discovered on their land, and white people wanted the land because it fulfilled our creed of materialism. We also learned in a way that we know only too well, that African-American slaves were brought in to work the gold mines. Our European ancestors stripped Native Americans of their land and their humanity, seeking to make the whole process *their* fault, assigning them blame for losing the land. We called them "savages" because they didn't understand the American creed, because they didn't understand how the real world works. Yes, we called them "savages," all the while killing them and forcing them off the land.

Does this all sound familiar? Housing in urban areas all over the country is being "redeveloped" as people with money take back urban land where poor people live, especially poor blacks and Latino people. A few years ago, we saw housing for 1,500 families demolished a mile from here in the name of redevelopment. The small protest over the destruction was met with the same line as was used to remove the Native Americans from that same land: they are bad people, unworthy of the land. Last fall, a few blocks from here, a subsidized housing project called McLendon Gardens was torn down in order to build expensive single-family dwellings. At least those developers were more honest. Rather than trying to blame those who were poor, they simply indicated that rich people wanted the land.

This is a familiar refrain throughout our country. White capital is "improving" the neighborhood, "revitalizing" the community, all the while blaming the "colored" folk who previously lived there for being dysfunctional and unable to succeed. It was this dynamic that Martin Luther King, Jr., came to understand, and he began to articulate a different vision. It was a vision that got him killed, but it was also the vision that gave him life and hope and possibility.

On this King Weekend we are asked to remember that vision and that hope, to remember that the struggle continues. To celebrate King Day is to remember and to give thanks for his life and his vision, to remember and give thanks for the lives and visions of all the people he represented, all the people who marched and sang and organized and who endured jail cells and firings and beatings and burnings and death. We give thanks for the witness of Martin Luther King, Jr., but we also give thanks that he was *not* the movement, that he was but one mighty wave on that river of justice.

We are now called to find our place in that great river, and if we think that we are small and insignificant, let us remember that even the mighty and uncontrollable Mississippi River begins as a small spring in its headwaters in Minnesota. In this image of justice flowing down like waters and righteousness like an ever-flowing stream, we can find our hope and our calling. There were witnesses called before Martin Luther King, Jr., and there are witnesses called after Martin Luther King, Jr.. On this day, we are being called to find our place in that river of justice, to join Dr. King and many others as witnesses to the God who has come to us in Jesus Christ to proclaim good news to the poor, freedom to the captives, to fling wide the prison gates to proclaim justice flowing like a mighty river. That is our source of hope on this day of remembering and celebrating and rededicating. God is calling us, too, to find our place in this river of justice. What should guide us in seeking the call of God in this time and in this place? No one put it better than Martin Luther King, Jr., on March 31, 1968, the Sunday before he was assassinated. He preached a sermon at the National Cathedral in Washington, D.C., called "Remaining Awake Through A Great Revolution," and this is part of what he said:

> *And I submit that nothing will be done until people of good will put their bodies and their souls in motion. And it will be the kind of soul force brought into being as a result of this confrontation that I believe will make*

the difference. Yes, it will be a poor people's campaign. This is the question facing America. Ultimately a great nation is a compassionate nation. America has not met its obligations and its responsibilities to the poor.[4]

Dr. King poses the question for us, the same question that Amos asked, the same question that Jesus asked: Who is our Lord? What rules our hearts? We can hear Amos calling to us. We can hear Jesus calling to us. We can hear Martin Luther King, Jr., calling to us. Let us respond as witnesses to God and let us find our place in that great river of justice. Amen.

---

1. James Melvin Washington, editor, *A Testament of Hope: the Essential Writings of Martin Luther King, Jr.,* (San Francisco: Harper and Row, 1986), from "I Have A Dream," p. 219.

2. We see this policy unfolding in our current Mid East policy, and in light of 9/11. See sermons 14 and 15 for more of this approach.

3. As this sermon was being preached, preparations were being made to inaugurate George W. Bush as president.

4. *Op. cit.*, Washington, p. 275.

To Whom Do We Belong?

The claim that we belong to God, a God who decisively determines our true identity amidst the competing claims upon our hearts and minds made by the idols of the world, is central to Stroupe's prophetic vision of the liberating call of the gospel in a world governed by the power of death. The following group of sermons, taken from various studies of New Testament texts, brings this claim and its consequences for Christian faithfulness sharply into focus. The dialectical complexity between good news and bad news in our journeys with the God of the Bible continues here as a consistent refrain. The claim that we belong to God is good news indeed, offering comfort and assurance. However, we often experience it as bad news to the extent that we want to belong to ourselves or allow ourselves to be defined by the idols of the world in our desire for a more palpable sense of security. Similarly, Stroupe does not fail to lift up the counter-cultural implications of this claim as he regards the church's relation to the life of the wider culture and nation.

Counter cultural

Church On The Outside:
Shall We Gather At The River?
Philippians 1:1-11; Acts 16:11-15
August 10, 1997

Our scripture passages for today chronicle a big step in the history of the church. In chapter 8 of Acts, we saw the movement of the gospel into Africa, and in chapter 16 of Acts, we see the movement of the gospel into Europe. The beginning of this movement occurs in Philippi, a leading city on the coast of Greece and an important Roman colony. The city of Philippi was named after Philip, the father of Alexander the Great. Just west of Philippi is the scene of one of the western world's most famous battles. After Brutus and Cassius led the assassination of Julius Caesar, they battle Marc Anthony and Caesar's nephew, Octavious, for control of Rome. The climactic battle took place near Philippi, and Brutus and Cassius are defeated. Octavious goes on to become Emperor Augustus, the first emperor of the Roman Empire, in whose reign Jesus is born. It is here in this famous and proud city that the gospel comes to Europe.

Well, it's not actually *in* the city of Philippi that the gospel comes to Europe. It was just outside Philippi, just outside the city walls that the gospel first comes to Europe. Just outside the city walls there is a group of women who gather for prayer on the Sabbath by the banks of the river. We don't know why they are gathering outside the city walls. Our text does not tell us, so it is an open question. Many commentators believe that they are not allowed to have a synagogue in the city, and thus they are not able to worship God in the city. They gather, then, at the river to worship God outside the city walls. If this is the case, where are the men? Why aren't they worshiping God with the women?

There is another explanation that is more feasible. I believe that the women wanted to worship in their own space, away from the men, and they gathered together outside the city walls. It is a daring move on their part. The city wall in Roman culture is the

105

dividing line between civilization and the wilderness. Inside the wall are the citizens. Outside the wall are the barbarians. The word in Latin for this city wall is "urb." It is the source of our word "urban" to describe the city. It is the wall that separates the citizens from the barbarians. So the women gather together in barbarian territory to pray. They gather at the river, outside the city walls.

Paul, Silas, and Timothy go to join these women. When Paul asks, "Shall we gather at the river?" he is not initiating a movement, he is joining a movement. Paul goes to speak to these women about Jesus Christ. Among the women is a woman named Lydia. The author of Acts, presumed to be the same person who wrote Luke's Gospel, tells us that God opened Lydia's heart while Paul is speaking. She becomes a convert to the gospel of Jesus Christ. She is the first recorded European to receive the gospel. Africa has already received the gospel earlier in Acts, and now in chapter 16, Europe receives the gospel.

The most obvious characteristic of Lydia is that she is a woman, and we must take a moment to recall that women at this time are seen as property of men. They have no humanity of their own. In the eyes of society, they receive their humanity, their legitimacy, through belonging to men — first their fathers, then their husbands, and if they outlive their husbands, then through some other male in their family, a son, a nephew, or an uncle. These women who gather outside the city wall however know something else. They know they are more than property of men. They long to find a new definition of who they are. They pray to God for their humanity and their identity and their dignity as people. I want to suggest that these women gather at the river as a revolutionary act, to seek to be who they are without worrying about what the men think about it; to give thanks to God that there are sisters in the city who see them as people, not as property or sex objects; to pray to God for a new definition, for freedom from their definition as property of men. So the question, "Shall we gather at the river?" is not only an evangelistic call, it is also a revolutionary call to dignity and justice.

As they pray outside the city walls, praying to God for freedom from being defined by men, the answer to their prayers comes in the form of a man. Here comes Paul to speak to these women. We can imagine their irritation and consternation as this *man* invades their prayer group on the banks of the river. Paul brings a surprising and welcomed message, however. He doesn't talk about women being property of men. Here at the river, outside the city walls, he talks about the glorious freedom of the children of God. He talks about each person having dignity in Jesus Christ. He talks about the categories of the world being broken down in Jesus Christ, categories like female and male, free and slave, rich and poor. These women hear a new message from this man. They don't hear the same old tired preaching that they have heard before, the preaching that seeks to bless and to strengthen the order of the categories of the world, whether it is in Judaism or Christianity. Rather, they hear a new and stunning message: the grace of Jesus Christ. In Jesus Christ they are not defined as property of men. In Jesus Christ they are defined as human beings, daughters of God! And Lydia is listening. We are reminded that Lydia is a seller of purple cloth, which means that she deals with wealthy folk who can afford her product. She is also the head of a household, and it likely means that she has considerable money herself. It is this money that has enabled her to break out of society's definition of who she is, as property of men. Because she has money, she can begin to think of herself as someone who is more than the property of a male. Lydia is an unusual woman in the Bible. She has the monetary power to struggle with society's view of her as a woman. When she gathers at the river on this day, she hears a stunning message of freedom, and the message comes *from a man*. She hears that she belongs first of all to God. She hears that she is somebody, not because she has money, but because God has claimed her in Jesus Christ. Because of that claim she is being redefined through the freedom that is hers in Jesus Christ.

Lydia is *listening*, and she is responding. Our text tells us that she is converted to the gospel, and she has her entire household baptized, as did Cornelius in chapter 10 of Acts. Her spiritual shift doesn't end there, however, because she also shifts in the view of money in her life. Money is the very thing that has helped her to begin to break away from the injustice of the world, and now she

107

begins to shift on how she views money. Instead of hoarding her money because of its power, she begins to share her money and to give it away. She does this because she has a new definition. Not a definition that money can buy, but a definition that the love and blood of Jesus Christ can buy. Now she opens her home to Paul, Silas, Timothy, and many others. Her home becomes the basis of the house church that will become the church at Philippi. It is this response of Lydia and others in Philippi, this response of joy and generosity that Paul came to love so much, a love that is evident in Paul's letter to the Philippians. If you haven't read that letter for a while, please go back and do so. It's only four chapters. That letter breathes with a sense of joy and generosity and possibility and vision and hope, gifts that Paul received from the women gathered at the river, including Lydia, who opened up her home and invited people in. We heard earlier some of Paul's words read to the house church at Lydia's home in Philippi.

> *I thank my God in all my remembrance of you, always in every prayer with joy, thankful for your partnership in the gospel from the first day until now. And, I am sure that he who began a good work in you will bring it to completion at the day of Jesus Christ.*
> — Philippians 1:3-6

Paul is "thankful for your partnership in the gospel from the first day until now." From the first day, that day on the riverbank, Lydia and her friends were struggling against the world's definition of women, a definition that denied their humanity. They gathered at the river, outside the city wall, outside the normal boundaries, out where the barbarians were. They gathered at the river. There, at the river, they sought to find help from God, to find their true definition. It was there that they received a vision of the glorious freedom of the children of God, the freedom they had in Jesus Christ.

The story of Lydia and her friends is the story of many of us, as we seek to find our way and our definition in a crazy and confusing world. We hear about all the pain and struggles there are in the world and in our lives. Pain and struggle in which we are stung and in which we participate. We long to find home. We hunger for the bread of life that will satisfy our hearts and our souls. We long for a definition that will allow us to express our passion for life and love and justice. It's not that we lack for definitions. There are many definitions that compete for our loyalty — gender, race, materialism, sexual orientation, nationality, economic class, educational level. The list of competing definitions goes on and on and on. Like Lydia, we sometimes find some measure of relief, some measure of freedom in some of those definitions. But these definitions also bring us oppression and exploitation and injustice, and they separate us from one another. And our hunger continues, our deep longing to find home, to be rooted in our true definitions.

Shall we gather at the river? Lydia and her friends had to go outside the boundaries to find relief, to go outside the city walls, to go out among the barbarians, to find their true definition. That is the case with many of us here at Oakhurst. We've gone outside the boundaries here, we've gone outside the city walls. We've gone into a place where we will encounter people whom the world tells us are barbarians, are enemies. Here, however, we don't find barbarians. Here we find something else, just as Lydia found on the banks of that river. Here we find a new definition of who others are. Here we do not find barbarians who will destroy us, not enemies with whom we battle to see who will get the most money or power, nor do we find strangers or sojourners. Here we find the glorious freedom of the children of God, and we are all redefined here. It doesn't matter what definitions we brought with us. We are all going to be redefined here. We will be redefined here as neighbors, friends, and partners, asked by God to become ambassadors of reconciliation in a world torn apart.

Shall we gather at the river? It is this definition of a new person — a new creation in Christ Jesus, as Paul calls it in a letter to another church in Corinth — which Lydia heard. It is this definition that changed her life and that made her an ambassador of reconciliation. She welcomed folk into her home and started a church there, a church that Paul came to remember so fondly, the church at Philippi. Shall we gather at the river? Can you hear that invitation today? Can you hear this new definition of each of us and of all of us? Can you hear what Lydia heard? Can you hear that this new definition is offered through the Spirit of our Lord Jesus Christ?

Shall we gather at the river? Can you hear that we are being redeemed this very moment, that we are being welcomed into the God movement through the grace and love of Jesus Christ? Can you hear that we are being asked to join in this God movement with Lydia and Paul and Julian of Norwich and Rosa Parks and Dorothy Day and all the witnesses who have gone before us? Can you hear that we are being asked to be redefined as children of God? Can you hear that we are being called to be witnesses ourselves, to share with others that same stunning, good news? Shall we gather at the river? Outside the boundaries, out where we think the barbarians are? Shall we gather at the river? Can we hear the calling from Lydia and Paul and the others? Shall we gather at the river? Amen.

A Child Of God
Psalms 139; Luke 12:22-34; Philippians 4:4-9
November 2, 1997

"Don't be afraid, little flock." That's a key verse in the passage from Luke. Jesus is aware how powerful fear is in our lives. Jesus knows that the power of fear can come to dominate us and can block God's grace in our lives. The emphasis here in the words that Jesus shares with his disciples is not that we shouldn't be afraid. All of us have fears and anxieties. The emphasis here is that we get into trouble when we let fear and anxiety define us. The result of such definitions is the kind of dehumanizing and alienating chaos that we are experiencing now in our culture. We are a people of fear, a culture of fear. We have burglar alarms and guns everywhere. We're afraid. We keep moving out of neighborhoods because people of whom we are afraid are moving into the neighborhoods. We are a culture of fear. Fear has become a commodity, a vehicle for selling items that will lessen our fears. Just watch the evening news, and you will see this marketing in process.

Some of us felt this power this past week with the stock market variations. I was amazed (I have trouble comprehending our culture) how much there was on television about the troubles of the stock market. There were news shows on again and again. I have trouble understanding this, just as I had trouble understanding why people were so fascinated with O. J. Simpson's white van going down the expressway. I do not understand why there was so much coverage of the stock market variations. And yet, I do understand it. Materialism rivals God in this culture for our loyalties, and if the stock market drops too much, our lives are in danger of losing their meaning. One of our central safeguards against the power of fear will be in jeopardy. It is also why a realistic and reasonable policy on gun safety is so difficult to achieve in this country. Guns are another rival for God in our culture. We must bow down to guns and the security that we believe that they bring to us, while our young people gun one another down in our streets.

There are many other definitions in our lives that rival God in our hearts. We know the litany well here at Oakhurst, and we recite it often: racial classification, gender, class, sexual orientation, nationality, and educational level, among others. We don't seek to deny how powerful these rivals are in our hearts. We confess how much we allow them to define us and dominate us. Here at Oakhurst, though, we try to do more than confess. We also seek to live out of another definition, all the while acknowledging how difficult it is to trust in this definition and to center our lives on it. What is that other definition? Well, this is what it is.

> If anybody asks you who I am, who I am, who I am, if anybody asks you who I am, tell 'em ...

Tell them what? "Tell 'em I'm a child of God." I know that I shocked you by singing it, so join with me this time.

> If anybody asks you who I am, who I am, who I am, if anybody asks you who I am, tell 'em I'm a child of God.

Okay. That's who we are, children of God.

The psalmist that we read this morning understood the struggle to trust in and to center our lives on this definition. In Psalm 139, we hear a different definition than the one that the world gives us.

> O Lord, you have searched us and known us. You know when we sit down and when we rise ... Where could we go to escape your Spirit? If we flew to the east or the west, you are there. For all these mysteries, for all your works, for the wonder of ourselves, we thank you! (paraphrased)

The definition that counts in our lives is that we are children of God. The psalmist gives praise to God that God has created us, that we belong to God, that God is always near in our lives. When we are able to hear this definition of ourselves, that we are children of God, then we can understand and begin to appropriate what Jesus says to his disciples in Luke. On one level, his words

112

seem so difficult. Don't be afraid for the next day. Don't worry about what you're going to wear. Don't worry about what you're going to eat. It sounds naive and unrealistic. "Don't be afraid, little flock." But there is so much to fear, inside ourselves and outside ourselves.

"Don't be afraid, little flock." Jesus is not trying to beat up on us, telling us how bad we are for worrying or for being afraid. He knows that we are worried. He knows that we are afraid. Instead of scolding us for our weakness, he is offering us a different view, another way to live. He is offering us a way to shift from being dominated by fear and anxiety. This other way is to hear, to receive, and to believe the good news: Don't be afraid, little flock, for it is God's good pleasure to give you good gifts. Don't be afraid, God wants to give you the gifts of the presence of God. God wants you to know the love and grace of God.

These words of Jesus in Luke are not naive ramblings of one who does not understand how the real world works. These words are stunning wisdom from one who has a profound experience of the presence of God. These words of Jesus, which he shares with his disciples, describe the realities of life, not the fantasies of idols like materialism. The fantasies of materialism tell us that if we get enough money and enough stuff, then we'll have our lives under control. That's fantasy. That's a lie. The reality of life is that we never have our lives under control, no matter what god we worship. The realities of life are that we must count on God to get us through very difficult times in our lives. The words of Jesus offer us a profound and deep sense of hope. "Don't be afraid, little flock." The God in whom we must trust is trustworthy — and not only trustworthy, but deeply desiring for us to trust him.

Paul emphasizes this approach in his words to the Philippians. "Don't worry about anything, the Lord is near." Paul emphasizes that our approach to life should be one of rejoicing and thanksgiving: "Rejoice in the Lord always." I'll say it one more time, "Again, I say rejoice." Why should we do this? Because God is near. "The Lord is near," Paul says, not talking so much about the Second Coming, not talking about Jesus coming back at the end of time. The Lord is near, at this moment, this morning. The Lord is near right now. That's what the psalmist lifts up. Where will we go that God won't be there? If we fly eastward to the sunrise or westward to the sunset, God will still be there. Where will we go to escape the presence of God? There is nowhere that we can go. Paul is talking about God here and now, right now, close to us. Paul is talking about where God lives, not way up in heaven, but in our midst, in *our* territory, here among us, looking for us, wanting to give us the gifts of the reign of God. Don't be afraid, for the Lord is near.

How do we do this? How do we move to find a sense of the closeness of God so that fear doesn't dominate our lives? I want to offer some clues this morning about moving into this realm, about affirming the sense that we are children of God, about affirming that the Lord is near, about moving away from the power of fear to dominate us. The beginning of this movement is to reflect upon what God has done for us. To begin in gratitude, as the cover of our bulletin for today says. "If the only prayer that we ever say in our whole life is, 'Thank you,' that would be enough." It is a quote from the great mystic Meister Eckhart. So we begin in gratitude. "Thank you, God, thank you!" I want to suggest that we begin this movement by practicing gratitude. Sometime today, perhaps before we celebrate the sacrament of the Lord's Supper — but, of course, not during the sermon — sometime today, let us think of something for which we are grateful to God.

I'm not talking about "oughtness" here. Don't focus on what you *should* be grateful for, don't focus on that. Focus instead on what you feel grateful to God for. Don't beat yourself up. Thank God for whatever it is, whatever you feel gratitude for, thank God for it, sometime today. You can say it in a prayer, you can sing it, you can dance it, and you can share it with someone else. But, this day, find a way to express gratitude to God for somebody or something that has occurred in your life. Just say, "Thank you."

Sometimes when I try this, all I can feel is "oughtness." I don't feel any gratitude in this process. In those times, I often beat myself up for being ungrateful, but I must also recognize that I simply don't feel grateful. If you don't feel like saying "Thank you," acknowledge that. Start there. Don't beat yourself up about how bad you are for not feeling grateful for all the gifts that you have, for all the people who have given you life. Rather, acknowledge where you are. "I don't feel grateful." Start there. Then think about it. Reflect on it. Why don't I feel grateful? Am I anxious? Am I bitter? Am I overwhelmed? Am I in pain? Am I angry? Am I disappointed? What keeps me from feeling gratitude? Again, don't beat yourself up. Don't say, "Oh, I should feel grateful, but I don't." Acknowledge the barrier. Acknowledge the blockage. That's a mighty big acknowledgment. If we can do that, we can take many steps in our lives. Our Sunday school class on spirituality and healing has been talking about the necessity of giving and receiving forgiveness in order to move toward health in our relationships to God and others. It's central. We know that it's not easy to acknowledge the blockage to gratitude. Why is it so powerful in my life? What am I afraid of? What am I mad about? Why can't I forgive? Why can't I feel forgiven? What keeps me from celebrating?

That is the first step in this movement away from fear and toward trust. To seek to give thanks out of gratitude, or to consider the barriers to gratitude in our lives. Then, "Take it to the Lord in prayer," as the song says. Have some time to receive God's presence. The Lord is near. There are many ways to experience God's presence, but our scripture and our tradition emphasizes that prayer is a central part of this journey. It's what Paul talks about in Philippians. So take some time this day for prayer. Indeed, take some time each day to lift up our gratitude to God, or to lift up the obstacles — what's blocking us? Take some time to lift up our fears, our hopes, and our dreams.

In the middle of our prayers, in the middle of our lives, let us listen for God, let us look for God. The Lord is near. Expect God in your life. Let us expect God in our lives, not to make everything go the way we want it to go. That's our usual image of God. If things go our way, we say, "Thank you, God." If things don't go our way, we say, "Where are you, God?" We don't need to expect God to be the magic wish granter. We're asked to expect God in our lives, to expect that there will be a sense of meaning in our lives, for we are part of a stream of grace, mercy, peace, and life.

Expect God in our lives. When the troubles come and attack us as they undoubtedly will, they can be seen as part of life, and we can develop communities where we assist one another and minister to one another in times of trouble. Or they can strike at the insecurities in our hearts, in those places where we're blocked, where we're vulnerable, where the idols are the most persuasive. "If I just had more money!" Lottery fever throughout this country is driven by the worship of money and our belief in its power to end our troubles. "If I could just win the lottery, my troubles would be over. Hey, I could help Oakhurst in its capital campaign!" I know how it feels. It's in these places that the idols speak to us, in these very places where we are so vulnerable and so afraid. It is into these places that we are asked to go in prayer. It is there that we have the opportunity to run to God, to ask for strength to have an appropriate response to our troubles, to keep from being dominated by idols in our troubles, to look for God's mercy and God's energy in our lives to keep us from being overwhelmed by our fears of falling into the abyss.

Don't be afraid, little flock. The Lord is near. We are children of God. It takes practice to receive this good news, to capture that sense of being a child of God, to allow the idea of the presence of God in our lives, to re-affirm that we are loved by God, that we are children of God. It takes a lot of practice. We're asked to practice it today and each day this week. The witness is clear. Lord, you know us and examine us. For many of us, that's a fearful statement, because it makes us fear that God is out to get us in order to crush us, to find that vulnerable place in our hearts, that place where we're needy. We are afraid that when God goes there, to the most confusing and confused places of our lives, God will say, "I don't love you." The psalmist does not mean it that way. The psalmist means, "Where could I go that you would not be? If I flew to the point of sunrise or westward across the sea, your hand would still be guiding me, your right hand holding me."

For all these mysteries, I thank you. For the wonder of myself, for the wonder of your works, I thank you. This is how the psalmist means it. That's how Jesus means it. That's how Paul means it. The Lord is near. If anybody asks you who you are, tell them, "I'm a child of God." Amen.

Between The Old And The New
John 20:24-31
April 19, 1998

He is known as "Doubting Thomas." Throughout the history of the church, he has come to be known as one who needs concrete proof. He certainly did doubt the testimony of the other disciples about the resurrection of Jesus. This morning, I want us to take a closer look at Thomas and his journey. If we do that, I think that we will have to re-appraise our assessment of Thomas. We will have to say "Thank you, Thomas." Thank you, Thomas — because he voices for us the feelings and thoughts that disciples have had throughout the ages in response to the news of the risen Jesus.

In John's Gospel we find that Thomas is an important member of the disciples. In the chapter 11, when Jesus is asked to go back to Bethany (which is close to Jerusalem) to raise Lazarus from the dead, there is a great fear among his disciples and in Jesus himself that he will be arrested by the leaders in Jerusalem and then executed. So Jesus waits a couple of days and finally decides to go to Bethany near Jerusalem. The disciples are afraid to go with him, but Thomas rallies them in chapter 11. He says, "Let's go also, so that we may die with him." We see that Thomas is a man of courage and dedication to Jesus.

When Jesus is with the disciples at the Last Supper in chapter 14 of John and again faces arrest, he tells them these famous words that we often hear in the church.

Do not let your hearts be troubled. Believe in God, believe also in me. In my Father's house there are many dwelling places. If it were not so, would I have told you that I go to prepare a place for you? And if I go and prepare a place for you, I will come again and will take you to myself, so that where I am, there you may be also. And you know the way to the place where I am going. — John 14:1-4

It is Thomas who responds to Jesus and who speaks for all the disciples and for all of us. "Lord, we don't know where you're going. How can we know where you're going? How can we know the way?" "I am the way, the truth, and the life," Jesus responded. The portrait of Thomas that emerges in John's Gospel is a portrait of a real person. At once courageous — "Let us go to Jerusalem and die with him!" At once bewildered — "Lord, we don't know where you're going." Though he disappears from the Bible after John's Gospel, he remained important to the early church. His name appears in the title of two books about the life of Jesus that did not make it into the Bible, the "Gospel of Thomas" and the "Acts of Thomas." For many centuries Thomas has been credited by the church for taking the gospel to India. Thomas, then, is an important figure for the early church and for us.

We must remember that the early church put the New Testament together. The four gospel accounts of the life of Jesus that the church chose to put in the Bible — Matthew, Mark, Luke, and John — do not have a trumpet-filled, triumphant chorus in response to the resurrection of Jesus. Rather, skepticism abounds. In Mark's Gospel, the women come to the tomb and hear that Jesus is raised from the dead. But Mark's Gospel ends with the disturbing news that the women do not say anything to anyone because they are so scared. Luke tells us that when the women finally get up the courage to speak, the men do not give their testimony much credence. The men believe that it's just the reaction of hysterical women who can't cope with the harsh realities of life, and as we see in chapter 20 of John, Mary Magdalene did not recognize the risen Jesus even when he stood in front of her and talked with her.

In light of these doubts described in the biblical accounts, we should not be surprised when Thomas won't accept the testimony of his brothers and sisters, "We have seen the Lord." Instead, he asserts that he must see it for himself. "Until I see it, until I touch it, I won't believe it." Though he is called Doubting Thomas, we should actually say, "Thank you, Thomas," for he reflects the realities of our lives in his struggles. Thomas reflects the depths of the power of death in our lives. Why wouldn't he believe? Why wouldn't he say "Yes"? Because things like the Resurrection don't happen in the real world. That's what Thomas believed, even after experiencing the power and the presence of Jesus in his earthly ministry. The reality is that death has deep and abiding power in the life of Thomas and in our lives. That's why Thomas said, "No." That's why we often say, "No," why we are unable to say, "Yes." Thomas says, "Unless I have an experience where I can touch the wounds myself, I will not believe." The power of death in the life of Thomas is so great that he must touch the wounds himself in order to believe.

Thomas reflects the realities of our belief struggles. The point here is not that believing makes it so. It's not that our faith or the faith of those first disciples makes the Resurrection true. The emphasis here is that the Resurrection points to another reality that's both *out there*, and that's *in here inside us*, another reality that we often don't encounter but that our faith wants to touch and to know. So when Thomas wants to touch that side and that wound, he speaks for all of us in our desire to know and to touch that other reality. We long for that other reality to be true, but we're so captured by the power of death that it hardly seems possible. It is this dimension that Thomas expresses for us when he says, "I will not believe until I can touch the wounds. I want to believe, but I can't believe." There is the deep longing for it to be true, but there is also the deep skepticism, expressed by Thomas, because of the power of death in our lives. So we can say, "Thank you, Thomas," for expressing what is in our hearts.

Jesus comes to Thomas and indicates that he knows the struggles that are in his heart. He appears to Thomas not to chastise him or to humiliate him in front of his friends. He doesn't appear to Thomas to scold him or to expose his feeble humanity. Rather, he appears to Thomas so that Thomas can believe, so that Thomas can begin the business of being a witness to the Resurrection. "Come on, Thomas, don't be overcome with doubt. Believe it, get on board, we've got work to do." Thomas says, "Yes, my Lord and my God." Thomas then becomes an important part of the story.

Thank you, Thomas, for witnessing to our story and our struggles. Because of the journey of Thomas, who longs for home but doubts that he will ever get there, his story is our story. We hope for the Resurrection, and we want it to be true, but we also know that death has power in our lives. Thomas' passion is that he really wants to believe in the Resurrection, but his problem is that he knows the reality of death. Jesus comes to him and offers him the opportunity of knowing the power of the Resurrection, the opportunity of finding a new reality, of finding life in the name of Jesus. Not just life after death, but life in *this* life. Jesus wants Thomas — and us — to perceive a new reality, not after we die, but right now; to live out of this new vision, not after we die, but right now.

This is where it gets tough. This is where the power of death raises its voice, as we seek to live the Resurrection *now*, rather than emphasizing the power of the Resurrection only after death. Risking to believe in life when we also believe that death has power.

I have had many experiences that reflect this struggle and the struggle of Thomas, and I want to share one of them with you now. Our daughter, Susan, just returned from a drama club trip to New York, a trip in which we were delighted. She loved the city of New York, and we may have created a monster there, I don't know. Her travels reminded me of my own experience of going to New York. It was life changing for me, an experience of the Resurrection for me, a sense of a whole new world out there for a country boy from Arkansas, a whole new reality.

But I almost didn't go. My good friend, David Billings, and I had done hard, manual labor the summer after our freshman year in college. After that we had pledged to find something else for the next summer, something less strenuous on our bodies, something we thought was more appropriate for guys going to college. We found a Presbyterian church in Brooklyn that needed workers for the summer program for youth in Bedford-Stuyvesant. We applied for it, and we were accepted! It was a stunning and exciting development. You can imagine two nineteen-year-old white boys from small-town Arkansas planning to go to New York City. We were excited!

But, before we left, it got complicated. It was a few days before we were to go, and we were sitting on the hood of David's car on a hot summer night in 1966, on a country road deep in the fields of Helena, Arkansas. It was only two or three days before we were to leave for New York, and I had to tell David that I wasn't going. I had gotten involved with a young woman in Helena, and I didn't want to leave her. Some of you have had that experience, I can tell by your laughter. I wanted to stay in Helena that summer and be with her. It was my first real romantic involvement, and I was really smitten. Love, and lust, had a hold on me. David and I talked a long time that night. I told him that I didn't think I could go to New York, that it would really hurt my heart to be away from this woman. He reminded me of the excitement that we had initially felt about going, about the opportunity of seeing a new world, of finding a whole new reality out there that we had not encountered in life on the delta of the Mississippi River. He spoke about being challenged and deepened by that world.

On that night — I give thanks — David prevailed. I did go to New York, and we both left home forever. It was a resurrection experience, a discovery of a whole new reality. It changed our lives. I thank God for my friend, David Billings, who persuaded me to try out the power of the resurrection. Like Thomas, I wanted to hold on to what I thought I knew. I knew that if I stayed on in Helena with this young woman, my life would be deepened, and I would be feeling wonderful. But I really didn't know what I thought I knew. I discovered later on, in an ironic twist, that she was dating another guy at the same time. So like Thomas, what I thought was real was not so solid after all. Again, I thank God for David who convinced me not to stay in the reality that I thought I knew, but to discover a new reality.

Jesus tells us earlier in John's Gospel that he has come to bring life and life abundant. That's what the Resurrection of Jesus Christ is all about, the opportunity to see and hear and touch a new reality. The risen Jesus is in our midst right now, calling to us, hoping for us, reaching out to us. Not to tell us how bad we are, how feeble we are, but to help us to say, "Yes," to come on in and to be about the business of witnessing to the Resurrection.

So, why don't we say "Yes"? Why don't we say, like Isaiah, "Here I am"? Because the power of death is so strong in our lives.

The story of Thomas reminds us how difficult it is for us to say, "Yes," to the risen Jesus. Like Thomas, we long for the power of the Resurrection, but like Thomas, we know the realities of the world. We are caught between the old and the new. We live in the midst of the powers of death. Thomas speaks about our doubts and our difficulties and our struggles. But Jesus speaks to us, too, as he did to Thomas. "Come on, Thomas, don't be overwhelmed by doubt. Touch me, and believe." The risen Jesus bids us, too, to open our eyes, to clean out our ears, and to ready our hearts for the great good news. There is life and life abundant, even in the midst of injustice and exploitation, even in the midst of the power of death, there is life, and life abundant.

Mary Magdalene said, "I have seen the Lord!" Many of the other disciples said, "We have seen the Lord!" Thomas finally says, "My Lord and my God." In this Easter season, in this time of the Resurrection, they all bid us to say, "Yes, we have seen the Lord!" They ask us to follow the risen Jesus into a new reality, here and now, to say, "Yes!" Thank you, Thomas. Amen.

Listening To The Dreams

These two sermons constitute the heart of Stroupe's homiletic response to the events of 9/11. They model how preaching can become a prophetic voice addressing the momentous events of the day through a deep and vital explication of scripture. These sermons also model the risk of following through on the counter-cultural implications of the gospel proclaimed: we belong to God as the true source of our identity and security. In a very specific and highly charged historical moment, Stroupe's prophetic voice speaks radically against the grain of the overwhelming chorus of cultural and political voices giving expression to the corporate sense of violation and vulnerability and the communal desire for retaliation and security. This chorus of voices was not limited to the general culture outside the doors of Oakhurst, but was echoed by many within the congregation of Oakhurst itself. As is clear throughout this collection of sermons, Stroupe's preaching is clearly informed by, and gives expression to, the distinctive voices of Oakhurst. However, these sermons demonstrate that the risk of prophetic speech modeled by Stroupe involves confronting the local congregation itself, as well as the culture and nation at large.

Comes The Dreamer
Genesis 41:1-36
November 4, 2001

Who among us has not been awakened by a scary and disturbing dream? Even young children are aware of these kinds of dreams.
We who are adults know it, also. It is a dream that leaves us full of
fear and anxiety, that shakes up our view of ourselves, and our
view of the world. No one is quite sure what dreams are. Freud
said that dreams are the repressed part of ourselves speaking to
the conscious part of ourselves. Jung said that dreams are the collective wisdom of the ages speaking to us. Wise people in many
cultures tell us that dreams are our ancestors speaking to us, or
perhaps even God speaking to us.

Whatever the nature of dreams, they have a way of helping us
to step outside ourselves, outside our normal way of perceiving
and thinking and understanding, helping us to gain perspective on
ourselves and our lives, and on life itself. That's why people like
Martin Luther King, Jr., used dream imagery in his most famous
speech in Washington, D.C. in 1963. "I have a dream," he said. He
was not talking about a dream that he had the night before. He was
talking about a vision of a new and different reality, a reality that
was difficult to imagine in the middle of white supremacy. A dream
that was nonetheless being imagined, a dream where racial classification would not be an essential component of life. "I have a
dream," he said, and that dream began to change the face and character of American society.

Whatever the nature of dreams, in today's scripture lesson we
see that one of the most powerful men in the world has a dream
that shakes him to the core. The great Pharaoh, king of the Egyptian empire, dreams about terrible things happening to his cattle
and his grain. These terrible things originate not in an alien source
outside Egypt, but from the great source of Egyptian fertility and
power, from the Nile River itself. So it is no wonder Pharaoh is
troubled and shaken by his dreams. The heart of the Egyptian

economy, livestock and agriculture are attacked, and they are attacked not by aliens but by the very symbol of Egypt. The Nile River is the source of the ugly ears and the lean cows that devour the good corn and the fat cattle. The Nile River becomes a place of death, not life, and the entire empire is shaken.

Pharaoh calls all of the wise leaders of his empire — his advisers, his visionaries. He calls the secretary of state, the secretary of defense, the secretary of commerce, but they cannot give him insight into his dreams. These advisers undoubtedly have interpretations of Pharaoh's dreams. After all, that is what they are paid to do, to interpret the meaning of what is going on. But none of these interpreters can speak to the trouble that occupies Pharaoh's heart. The best and brightest of the empire are stumped, and their vision is truncated. They cannot see what these dreams mean.

They are stumped because these dreams call into question the very reality that Pharaoh and Egypt think they know. Because these dreams attack the heart of the Egyptian empire, no one whose reality depends upon Egypt's view of life is able to interpret these dreams. The best wisdom of Egypt is useless.

That brings us to a hinge point in this story, indeed in the entire Old Testament history of Israel. Pharaoh's cupbearer remembers a promise that he made to somebody in prison, to a foreigner in jail. He remembers that he had promised to remember this prisoner when the right time came, but it has been two years since his release from prison, and he has forgotten his promise. But now he remembers, and he confesses to Pharaoh that he has made a mistake. He tells Pharaoh that he remembers a Hebrew prisoner who is a visionary, a dreamer. Pharaoh is wise enough to send for the prisoner.

We must not underestimate Pharaoh's wisdom in seeking the advice of this young Hebrew prisoner. Pharaoh, one of the most powerful men in the world, could have dismissed the cupbearer's suggestion as idiotic. How can a foreigner, a prisoner, a convicted sex offender bring wisdom to the great Pharaoh? What can this prisoner discern that the great, wise leaders of Egypt have not discerned? Yet, to his credit, he sends for this young Hebrew named Joseph.

We must take a moment and notice how highly unusual this is. Almost always, dreamers and visionaries are greeted with skepticism and often with contempt. We have seen this earlier in the Joseph saga. Just before the boy Joseph is thrown into a pit the first time — not by a foreigner, but by his brothers — they say with contempt, "Here comes the dreamer." Dreamers and visionaries are often seen as naive, as unrealistic, not understanding the real world and how it works. Sometimes they are seen as threatening because they are able to see deeper and longer. They see beneath the surface of what we call "real." They are able to see root causes and a deeper understanding of life. They are able to see long-term consequences of actions long before most of us even notice the action, much less the consequences. They're able to see beneath the surface of existing systems.

In 1963, when Martin Luther King, Jr., said, "I have a dream," white society thought he was ridiculous. He was considered to be a communist, a threat to the social order. Though he was no communist, he was a threat to the existing social order of white supremacy. He envisioned a new reality in which white people would not be on top. He envisioned a reality in which humanity would be a family instead of a hierarchy with white people on top. And in today's scripture story, comes another dreamer. Nothing could be more ridiculous or outlandish than this scene that is given to us in chapter 41 of Genesis: the powerless prisoner Joseph, a foreigner, standing before one of the most powerful people in the world. Joseph is there because he has been summoned as a dreamer and a visionary.

We must also note Joseph's demeanor here. He has learned a lot in prison. He knows his strengths. The narrator in Genesis tells us that before he goes to see Pharaoh, he cleans himself up. He's good looking, and he's charming, and he wants to make sure that Pharaoh sees that. He knows how to get his message across. Joseph also knows his weaknesses. His two "pit stops" have taught him about his weaknesses. No prancing around here, as he did with his brothers, telling them how great he was. In today's story, he doesn't even take credit for his visions. When Pharaoh says to him, "I've heard that you have a gift for interpreting dreams," Joseph discounts himself and says, "It's not me. It's God. God will give the interpretation if God chooses." He gives the credit to God and not to himself. His two times in the pit, in exile, has humbled and deepened him.

Through God's power, Joseph the outcast, the prisoner, the powerless one, offers profound insight into Pharaoh's dream. Joseph is able to interpret the dreams because he stands outside the value system of the Egyptian empire. To him, the Nile is just another river and is not the source of creativity and life that it is to the Egyptians. He brings wisdom and insight to the dilemma of Pharaoh and Egypt. He is able to see root causes and discern long-term consequences. Comes the dreamer, and he brings truth and discernment.

Pharaoh and Egypt are shaken to their core by these dreams. The central symbols of their reality are attacked — cows and crops and the Nile River. The discernment of Joseph through God's power helps Egypt avoid great disaster. Prior to Joseph's discernment, all of Egypt is shaken and afraid. We know that feeling in our country. In many ways, we in the United States find ourselves in the same predicament as Pharaoh was after September 11. Our predicament is not a dream. We've seen thousands killed in our country. But in many ways, we are like Pharaoh and Egypt. The attackers of September 11 used our airplanes to carry out the attack. Our airplanes, symbols of our economic and military power now used as implements of destruction, now becoming symbols of death rather than economic power. None of us can trust getting on an airplane right now, and none of us can trust airplanes coming toward us. Our military now has standing orders to shoot down our own commercial airplanes. Our view of ourselves as a superpower able to control the world with our economic and military power has been interrupted and not only interrupted, but severely shaken.

Like Pharaoh, our leaders have called in their wise advisers, their interpreters — the secretaries of state and of defense and of commerce and all kinds of other visionaries — to help them interpret the meaning of these events and this predicament. What does it mean? The most commonly accepted interpretation given is that innocent Americans were attacked by fanatical, if not insane, terrorists, those who are haters of America and the freedom, equality, and opportunity of the modern world that it represents. The course of action that follows from this interpretation is to kill or imprison the terrorists, even if it means destroying towns and civilians to do it. Indeed, that is our present interpretation and course of action. Our symbols of power and might, like Pharaoh's symbols, have been attacked, and our response is to attack in return.

In our struggles and in our present interpretation and actions, we must be very careful to remember this biblical story of Pharaoh and Joseph. Pharaoh was wise enough to discern that the predicament was too profound and too threatening to leave the interpretation of it to the powerful. It is no surprise that our president calls in Donald Rumsfeld, John Ashcroft, and Dick Cheney or that the previous president called William Cohen and Janet Reno. They are trusted advisers and should be consulted. What this biblical story of Pharaoh and Joseph tells us, however, is that the interpretations of these powerful people are not helpful in the situation because they are so aligned to the symbols of our culture that their visions are truncated.

This biblical story tells us that because this situation is so threatening, the powerful will not be able to interpret it well. In order to discern the truth, we must turn to those who are powerless as Joseph was. We must turn to those who are not greatly invested in the system that is so threatened. The dreamers and the visionaries, like Joseph, are the ones who must be consulted to help us interpret our predicament. They will be able to discern deeper truths in this situation, truths that the powerful cannot discern. Now, of course, the dreamers and the visionaries are going to be seen as naive and unrealistic. To believe that we must not answer violence with violence is seen as unrealistic and even as treason. But we must listen carefully to this biblical story in Genesis. Our future depends upon our listening to the dreamers and the visionaries in our midst. In today's story in Genesis, the future of Pharaoh and Egypt depended upon the system listening to the dreamer. So does ours.

Where are the Josephs of our day and our time? Oh, they are in our midst — those who are poor, who are in prison, who are powerless, who are oppressed and outcast. Many have been crushed by their oppression and marginality, but some are like Joseph. They have developed the capacity to see deeper realities, and they see more than Islamic fundamentalists in our current predicament. They see Islamic fundamentalists, but they see more than that, and that is what we need to hear. Where are the Josephs? They are in our midst, and next week we will look at some of them and seek their insights and interpretations.

For today, as we tremble before the approach of another week, as our leaders contemplate whether we will bomb during the holy season of Ramadan in Afghanistan, we must ask ourselves, "Will we be wise enough to listen to the dreamers and visionaries in our midst?" Pharaoh sent for Joseph. Joseph didn't invite himself into Pharaoh's presence, that's not how it is done. Pharaoh sent for Joseph. Will our leaders do that? Will we send for people like Joseph? Or will we say with contempt as Joseph's brothers did, "Comes the dreamer," naive, unrealistic, doesn't know how the world really works.

There is an alternative to this contempt. Will we say with Pharaoh — the one we would least expect to do it — will we say with desperation and longing and hope, "Comes the dreamer!" Come, help us discern the deeper meaning, the deeper realities which our truncated vision prevents us from seeing. We are at the watershed point in our history. This is not a game. This is fundamental. In the midst of tragedy and death, God is moving in our history. Like Pharaoh and Egypt, we are at a crucial turning point. Whose voices, whose interpretations will we heed? The court advisers? The powerful? Or the dreamers like Joseph? It is a hinge point in our history. The future of our children and our grandchildren await our decision. Let us remember this biblical story, and let us listen to the dreamers. Amen.

Seeing Beneath The Surface
Genesis 41:37-57
November 11, 2001

As we read in our scripture lesson for today, Pharaoh has had dreams that have shaken him and the Egyptian empire to their core. The symbols of Egyptian power and wealth — cows and corn and the Nile River — are attacked in dreams. Pharaoh calls for the secretary of state, the secretary of defense, and Alan Greenspan, the head of the Federal Reserve, to help him interpret the situation. What's going on here? They have many things to tell him, but none of them strike Pharaoh as being true. There's still something missing. He has not heard what he needs to hear in order to understand the true meaning of these dreams. In his desperation, he turns to a foreigner, a Hebrew prisoner named Joseph.

Joseph tells Pharaoh that these dreams mean that seven years of plenty are coming, followed by seven years of famine. When Joseph tells Pharaoh this interpretation, it strikes home for Pharaoh. He is both pleased and astonished. He has found a visionary, someone who is able to see beneath the surface of Egyptian society, someone who is able to see deeper realities and powers that are often hidden from most of us because we are so caught up in the values of our systems. When crisis comes, we are unable to respond well because these deeper realities are hidden from us. Pharaoh finds a visionary who is able to see these realities.

Pharaoh receives these insights, and he does a highly unusual thing. He makes a radical change in his public policy because he has discerned the truth of these deeper realities. He puts the visionary in charge of re-ordering the Egyptian way of life. We must recall that this visionary is a prisoner, convicted of a sex offense. It is as if President Lyndon Johnson called Martin Luther King, Jr., on April 3, 1968, to tell Dr. King that he wanted to put him in charge of the Justice Department of the United States. Not the Martin Luther King, Jr., who has been sanitized by our national holiday, but the King who was so threatening to the American way

131

of life that he was jailed almost thirty times and was finally assassinated on April 4, 1968, as he came to Memphis to help striking garbage workers seek living wages. It is an astonishing development in Egypt, that Pharaoh brings a foreigner out of prison to become the number two person in charge of the Egyptian empire.

It is a stunning development for Joseph. From the pit he comes, a dreamer and a visionary, but also a prisoner and a foreigner who becomes the head of the Egyptian government, answering only to Pharaoh. I can think of only one comparable rise in modern times, Nelson Mandela's rise in South Africa. He was not a foreigner as was Joseph, but to most white people in South Africa, he was a foreigner, a huge threat to their way of life. Yet after 27 years in prison, Nelson Mandela rises to become president of South Africa, a pivotal figure at a pivotal time.

Pharaoh shows wisdom. He recognizes the limits of the Egyptian empire, a recognition that is unusual in itself for kings. He calls on a visionary to help discern and to help implement the realities revealed in Pharaoh's dream. Pharaoh was shaken by his dreams. It was such a deep and disturbing threat that he was forced to open his ears and his heart to receive the voice of a visionary who was outside the circle of the powerful. The deep realities that would shape Egypt for the next fifty years could be seen only by one who was not heavily invested in the Egyptian system.

We have had that same experience in this country since September 11. The attacks of September 11 have shaken us to our core. The advice from the powerful is the same that it has always been and the same that it will always be. In the Cold War, it was the communists. In the new century, it is the terrorists. It has reinforced the conservative ideology that the world is a dangerous and threatening place. It has reinforced the idea that our lives must be based on protecting ourselves from being contaminated by others. In this atmosphere, everyone becomes a suspect. We are now holding over 1,000 people in our jails without specific charges. It is the most that we have jailed without specific charges since we rounded up people of Japanese descent in World War II. We should not be surprised at this reaction by our leadership. After all, the Bush administration began its term by renouncing treaties on global warming and a missile defense system, indicating that we were a people on our own, an island to ourselves. The current administration also attacked the common good by pushing a tax relief bill that only helped rich and comfortable people, and now we are beginning to pay the price for it.

However, it's not just the conservatives who can't see the deeper realities. Many of us are so threatened that we, too, get caught up in the fear. One of my favorite columnists, Leonard Pitts, who writes for the *Miami Herald*, has sounded like a writer for Jesse Helms since September 11. People who are normally moderate like Jonathan Alter, a columnist in *Newsweek*, lambasted those visionaries among us who sought to discern deeper realities. He called them "Blame America Firsters" and dismissed them as fools. This is part of that column.

> *And none but a fool would say, as the novelist Alice Walker did in* The Village Voice, *that "the only punishment that works is love." We've tried turning the other cheek. After the 1993 World Trade Center bombing we held our fire and treated the attack as a law-enforcement matter. The terrorists struck again, anyway. This time the Munich analogy is right: appeasement is doomed.*
>
> *America Firsters grasped this point after Pearl Harbor and the isolationists ran off to enlist. So why can't Blame America Firsters grasp it now? Al Qaeda was planning its attack at exactly the time the United States was offering a Mideast peace deal favorable to the Palestinians. Nothing from us would have satisfied the fanatics, and nothing ever will. Peace won't be with you, brother. It's kill or be killed.*[1]

These are the kind of times in which we live, the kind of times when dreamers and visionaries are seen as naive and unrealistic and even as traitors. When Congresswoman Cynthia McKinney suggests that Mideast realities are connected to September 11, she is branded as a traitor in this country. Those who see an endless cycle of violence in Afghanistan that threatens to spiral out of control are dismissed as unrealistic in the real, dangerous, and threatening world. Those who suggest that our participation in injustice in the Mideast and other parts of the world is connected to September 11 are called naive at best and traitors and un-American at worst. Difficult to hear. Difficult words to speak. Yet, like Pharaoh in Egypt, we would be well advised to listen to the Joseph's in our midst, to the dreamers and the visionaries. In their dreams and perceptions we will glimpse the redeeming activity of God in a terrible time. I've compiled a list of some of the insights from dreamers and visionaries in our midst. Folks like Martin Luther King, Jr., Dorothy Day, June Jordan, Wendell Berry, Michael Lerner, and many others. I want to share five insights culled from their work. You may not agree with all of them. Indeed, you may not agree with any of them. Some of our members have called me un-American because of my sermons on the issues of September 11. But, I hope that these visionaries will provoke all of us to go beneath the surface, to compile our own lists of insights and revelations.

In the midst of a terrible time, I want to share five insights from dreamers and visionaries in our midst. The first insight is that we in the United States are part of the world. That seems obvious in stating it, but many of us in this country believe that we are above the rest of the world, if not in control of the world. We somehow have developed the belief that we are aloof from the rest of the world. It is a difficult lesson for us to learn. Our president began his term by renouncing the treaty on global warming, indicating that we were aloof from this threat to the world community. He also renounced the treaty on the missile defense system, which has kept nuclear weapons out of the air. He indicated that we would go our own way on this. The events of September 11 should remind us that we are part of the world, no matter how much we would like to think otherwise.

It is one of the lessons that Joseph had to learn in order to grow up. He was his daddy's favorite, and he made sure that his siblings knew it. His attitude changed but only because of his time in exile, in the pit and in prison. He learned that he was part of a larger community. I was an only child growing up, and I felt that the world centered on me. There are many blessings of being an only child, but one of the curses is that one has trouble not focusing only on the self. I remember when I graduated from high school, I had this fantasy that the school would close down after I left, that its history was essentially over. I've noticed that somehow they've managed to go on without me. I also remember that when our second child was born, I was sad for our first child. He would no longer be an only child. He would not be able to receive the same amount of attention from my wife and me that he had been receiving, and he would feel the loss. Yet, I also felt good for him, because he would necessarily be forced to see that the world did not center on him. His sister would, and did, shift his worldview.

I believe that we have the same opportunity now as a nation. In many ways before September 11, we thought of ourselves as only children in the world of nations. We believed that the world centered on us. Now we see that there are siblings out there, and that we must learn to live together. If we do not learn to live together as sisters and brothers, the consequences will be drastic. Not just for them, but for us, too.

The second insight is to understand the way the rest of the world sees us, and to be frank in that assessment. They see us as a greedy empire. There is no other way to put it. Some of them may envy us, but most of them see us as an empire that sucks money and labor and resources from other cultures, as an empire that has the military might to back up this system. They see us as believing that money is life, that money is God. That's the way most of the world sees us. They may not tell us that directly because they want stuff from us, but most of the world sees us as a greedy empire.

Our own president seems to be gaining insight on this perception. He alluded to it in his speech in Atlanta. He said, "Too many have the wrong idea of Americans as shallow, materialist consumers who care only about getting rich or getting ahead."[2] He has been listening to some Joseph in his midst. I don't know who it is, but I'd like to think that it is Condoleezza Rice, since she is Presbyterian.

The third insight is that while we must protect ourselves in the short run, we must recognize a longer view. Those who organized the attacks of September 11 are a threat to us and to humanity. They are smart and dangerous, and they must be contained. We must recognize, however, that in the long run, we will not be able to bomb them away. The only way that we will have protection in the long run is to make sure that we are working for justice as a nation and that other nations are moving toward justice. If we pursue this course there will be no Afghanistan or Saudi Arabia or other nations that will harbor these folk because they believe that they are fighting against injustice. We must recognize that in the long run the only real protection we have is to do what Pharaoh did and change our perception of reality. In our case, such a change will mean a shift of energy toward justice and peace and away from dominating the world and away from believing that affluence and individualism are the primary goals of life.

That leads to the fourth insight. We must use the same amount of energy that we are using in Afghanistan to work for a just peace in the Middle East. We must make it clear to Israel that the Palestinians need a homeland and make it clear to the Palestinians that Israel will exist. This fourth insight may sound impossible, but in 1993-1995, when Yitzak Rabin was the leader of Israel, he was working for peace. During this time there were few acts of Palestinian violence toward Israel. There was one central act of violence during this time, and it took Rabin's life. This violence came not from a Palestinian terrorist, but from a right wing Israeli terrorist, and it ended the time of relative peace in the Middle East.

We must re-focus our understanding of justice and sharing. We have turned a deaf ear and a hard heart to our hoarding of most of the world's resources. We have indeed touted globalization and have demanded that other people give us their resources and their labor and their capital so that we can live better lives, all the while telling them that they will live better lives. That brings us to the fifth insight. We must have a reformation here at home. We must turn away from our idolatrous worship of the free market that requires universal pollution, produces global warming, promotes greed as a virtue, increases geometrically the gap between the rich and the poor, and which needs a strong military to enforce this belief system. We must turn away from that and turn toward loving and engagement and community. We must turn away from believing that money is life. If we do not, the events of September 11 will happen again and again, the consequences of our idolatrous worship.

In this area, once again, a Joseph seems to be getting the ear of President Bush. Initially, after September 11, he told us that the answer for us was to go shopping while the military killed the terrorists. I think that Bill Clinton would have said the same thing, so let no one hear me criticizing the president just because he's a Republican. The point here is that those in power have difficulty perceiving the deeper realities and hearing different voices that point to those deeper realities.

In his Atlanta speech, President Bush seemed to float a trial balloon for a different view, telling us to get involved, indeed telling us to serve.

> *Ours is a wonderful nation full of kind and loving people, people of faith who want freedom and opportunity for people everywhere. One way to defeat terrorism is to show the world the true values of America through the gathering momentum of a million acts of responsibility and decency and service.*[3]

He's on to something there. That is the way that we will defeat terrorism in the long run, by moving from a model of individualism and self-sufficiency to a model of community and interdependence. It remains to be seen what kind of leadership our president will give us, but I recognize that God is great. Just as God transformed Abraham Lincoln, another Republican in a difficult time, so may God transform George W. Bush. I pray that God will.

Whatever our leaders tell us and wherever our leaders seek to take us, these must be our guiding values. First, we must recognize ourselves as children of God. That's who we are. That's our primary definition. And the second value is like unto it. We must recognize others as children of God. That's their primary definition. I've read many articles on the September 11 events. Some of them have been awful. Some of them have been very challenging to me. Some of them have been very insightful. Of all of them, I want to return to my longtime mentor, Wendell Berry, to hear some words from him on our current predicament:

> *In a time such as this when we have been seriously and most cruelly hurt by those who hate us, and when we must consider ourselves to be gravely threatened by those same people, it is hard to speak of the ways of peace and to remember that Christ enjoined us to love our enemies, but this is no less necessary for being difficult. Even now we dare not forget that since the attack of Pearl Harbor — to which the present attack has been often and not usefully compared — we humans have suffered an almost uninterrupted sequence of wars, none of which has brought peace or made us more peaceable. The aim and result of war necessarily justifies the violence that won it and leads to further violence. If we are serious about innovation, must we not conclude that we need something new to replace our perpetual "war to end war"? What leads to peace is not violence but peaceableness, which is not passivity, but an alert, informed, practiced and active state of being. We should recognize that while we have extravagantly subsidized the means of war, we have almost totally neglected the ways of peaceableness. We have, for example, several national military academies, but not one peace academy. We have ignored the teachings and the examples of Christ, Gandhi, Martin Luther King, and other peaceable leaders. And here we have an inescapable duty to notice also that war is profitable, whereas the means of peaceableness, being cheap or free, make no money. The key to peaceableness is continuous practice.*[4]

This is an exhausting and difficult list of insights, and there are other helpful insights, but I've run out of time. I hope that each of us, whether we applaud these insights or whether they make us boil with anger, will take the time to go beneath the surface and look at the deeper realities. Like Pharaoh in Joseph's time, we have been thrust into a terrible nightmare, full of dread and anxiety. But there are Josephs in our midst, visionaries and dreamers who can help us chart our course to health and safety. May we find those Josephs and listen to their insights.

This Pharaoh in Genesis 41 listened to Joseph, and his nation turned a terrible situation into a blessing for all people. Another Pharaoh, generations later, whose story is found in Exodus, did not listen to the visionary in his midst, a visionary named Moses. That Pharaoh saw his army obliterated in the sea. We, too, are in the same difficult times as were those Pharaohs in Egypt. The visionaries and dreamers like Joseph and Moses call us to see the deeper realities. There is no long-term protection other than justice and peace. Every book in the Bible proclaims this in one way or another. All of our Christian tradition emphasizes this again and again and again. There is no long-term protection other than justice and peace, centered in the God of all creation. Those voices are calling to us now in a difficult time. Let us hear them. Let us heed them. Let us believe them. Let us live them. Amen.

1. Jonathan Alter, "Blame America Firsters," *Newsweek*, October 15, 2001.

2. "Bush: Courage, optimism will guide America," *The Atlanta Constitution*, November 9, 2001.

3. *Ibid.*

4. Wendell Berry, "Thoughts in the Presence of Fear," October 23, 2001, Internet Communications.

Benediction

This sermon, on the confrontation between the prophet Nathan and King David, and the sermon on Mary's confrontation with Jesus in the garden that opens the book, function together as thematic bookends of the collection as a whole. Hearing our names called by the risen Jesus is to come alive to the new reality of God's future amidst a world gripped by the power of death. Consequently, this new life open to the reality of God's future is fleshed out as a witness to God's justice in the face of the various social, political, and economic structures of power holding sway in our neighborhood, city, nation, and world. Stroupe is clear, however, that this call to witness heard in the call of the risen Jesus also entails a demand for confession on the part of the church because of its own long and continuing history of complicity with the principalities and powers of the world. The church must continually pray for discernment in judging when it is called to proclaim and when it is called to confess.

Truth Speaks To Power
2 Samuel 12
August 15, 1999

On a hot day, on Wednesday, August 28, 1963, more than 250,000 people gathered by the Lincoln Memorial in Washington, D.C. to celebrate the American vision of equality and to demand equal rights for black people in the United States. It was during this gathering that Martin Luther King, Jr., gave his most famous speech, "I Have A Dream." Less than three weeks later, on Sunday, September 15, 1963, white America answered. A bomb blew up Sixteenth Street Baptist Church in Birmingham, injuring many and killing four little girls, dressed in their Sunday best for church.

The cries went out across the nation: Why the children? Why harm children? We heard those cries again this week as another white person — a white man — shot up a Jewish day care center in Los Angeles. Why the children? Who kills children? It should be obvious by now. Our society is intertwined with, and rooted in, guns and violence, and children will not be deemed exempt from that identity. When we deny the humanity of others, when we believe in violence as the answer, it won't stop with adults. Our children will be killed in this kind of society. It's terrible.

Unfortunately, it's not new. I became an adult in an era of violence and killing — four dead children in Birmingham. Two months after they were blown up, the President of the United States, John Kennedy, was assassinated. Scores of people were murdered in the Civil Rights Movement, and hundreds more were injured. In January, 1965, Malcolm X was assassinated, and in June, 1966, James Meredith was shot. Dr. King himself and Robert Kennedy were assassinated within two months of one another in 1968. It is a litany of the worship of guns and violence, whether it's 1848 or 1968 or 1999. What makes us think that our children will be exempt from the consequences of our worship? Indeed, we are teaching our children the catechism of violence, as we glorify it on television, in movies, and in video games.

143

Our biblical story for today reminds us of that difficult lesson. Bathsheba is exploited, Uriah is murdered, David is exposed, and the child dies. There are no exemptions. It reminds us of the difficult consequences that ensue when we deny the humanity of others and when we use violence to enforce that denial. We know this story. If you know anything at all about David, you know about a giant named Goliath and a beautiful woman named Bathsheba. David takes Bathsheba, the wife of another man, and uses her, and then he murders her husband Uriah to cover it up. We aren't prepared for this side of David.

We see David's raw power as king. It is a power that is unchecked. Jonathan is not around to tell David to cool it, to hold his power in check. Jonathan is dead, killed in war. David has no peer who will speak up to him. So his power is out of balance. He exploits Bathsheba as a woman and kills her husband to cover it up. He believes that he has gotten away with it. Bathsheba doesn't know about David's scheme. Uriah does not know that he carries his death sentence in the very letter that David tells him to deliver to Joab. Only Joab, David's army commander, has some hint as to what David is doing in this story.

The biblical story, however, tells us that God knows, and God sends a prophet to speak to David. Truth must speak to power. God sends the prophet Nathan to speak the truth to the powerful David. Nathan is not unknown to David. Back in chapter 7, Nathan came to the court to bless David's reign. When Nathan shows up this time, we don't know what David is thinking, but we do learn that Nathan has come this time for a different purpose — not to bless David's reign, but to call it into question. Truth must speak to power.

Nathan has been around the king's court, though, and he doesn't just burst in and tell David that he has sinned grievously. Nathan knows that it is a dangerous situation. Instead, he tells David a story about a rich man and a poor man. The rich man abuses the poor man and his little lamb, and as David hears the story, his anger rises. After all, he used to be a shepherd boy himself. He has learned about taking care of sheep and lambs. His anger and indignation rise, and he becomes like many of us Christians in the

144

church. He is judgmental and superior, and he is ready to crush this mean, dirty sinner. "Where is this man? He deserves to die! I'll get my elite bodyguard to torture him until he restores the poor man. Where is this man?" Nathan's strategy has worked. He has engaged David with this story and has brought David into the story. "Where is this man?" Then comes the shattering focal point of Nathan's story, "You are the man."

Truth speaks to power. It's a stunning and dangerous moment in biblical history. "You are the man." How will David react? Will he strike down Nathan as he struck down Uriah? As those white folks in Birmingham struck down the four little girls in Birmingham, as the white man struck down those children in the Jewish day care center this week? It's a dangerous moment when truth speaks out. We often think that the truth is wonderful, but when truth speaks out, it's dangerous. And this is a dangerous moment in biblical history. "You are the man."

To David's credit, he does not strike down Nathan. Rather, he shows the depths of his humanity, and this depth of humanity is one of the main reasons that Israel remembers him with such fondness. Not because he's good but because he's real. He's a human being. He doesn't try to evade Nathan or God or himself. He confesses. "I have sinned against the Lord." Interestingly enough, he doesn't say, "I have sinned against Bathsheba. I have sinned against Uriah." That reluctance will cost him dearly. Nathan tells him that his house will know violence for the rest of its existence. David does confess however, that he has abused his power. His confession is all the more remarkable because he is the king. He has absolute power. It's a model of public leadership that is desperately needed but rarely ever followed.

This week also marks the twenty-fifth anniversary of the resignation of Richard Nixon as president in 1974. It all began because Nixon would not confess his knowledge of the Watergate break-in. Had he admitted it straight up, he would have remained president of the United States. He could not bring himself to confess. We've seen that same story played out again in the last two years with President Bill Clinton. How much would we all have been spared if President Clinton had told us in January 1998, "I

145

did have sexual relations with Monica Lewinski"? Clinton could not bring himself to confess, and the struggle stretched out over eighteen months. A lot of people are still disgusted with him and with Al Gore, the vice president. We may get George Bush and the dangerous Republican right wing in the White House because of Clinton's connection with Gore, because of Clinton's failure to be the kind of leader that we needed him to be, and because of Clinton's failure to confess his violation of the public trust.

David does confess, however. He redeems Israel with his confession, and it's because God sent a prophet to David to speak the truth to power. Truth must speak to power. That's one of the lessons of this difficult story in 2 Samuel. Nathan is sent by God to remind King David that the purpose of his kingship, that the purpose of having power, that the purpose of government is not to keep rich folk in power, but rather to establish justice. That's the reason God ordains government, not to establish order so much as to establish justice. Nathan is sent by God to remind David that even the king, the absolute power, is framed by justice. Especially in Israel, where Yahweh is the center, the king must be framed by justice.

Truth must speak to power. Power unchecked and unbalanced leads to incredible abuses, as we see in this story, as we see in the history of white supremacy that has so often been unchecked. It's why Presbyterians have great distrust of centralized power. It's why we don't have any bishops. It's why we prefer a system of checks and balances. I was reminded of this recently in a matter that came before our church's governing board, the Session. It was a matter that I handled badly. I tried to make an end run around the Session because I knew that they wouldn't approve what I wanted them to approve. The matter did come to light at the Session meeting, and the Session, of course, turned it down. One of the elders on the Session later told me that they did not want to be a "Yes" person for me on the Session. They preferred to be the elder that the congregation had elected them to be, and I needed to remember that. It was a painful but necessary reminder for me of why we Presbyterians greatly distrust centralized power.

Power needs a prophetic voice in order to govern well, in order to provide justice. There must be prophetic voices speaking to power. Power needs prophets. Power doesn't like prophets, but power needs prophets. It's why we must speak out on issues of guns and violence in our society. It's why we must march and cry out to powerful people about the need for decent health care for the poor. It's why we must stand against the theory of white supremacy that's held not only in the KKK and the Aryan Nations but also in the corporate boardrooms and the individual white bedrooms around this country. That's where the origins of white supremacy are. Its origins are not in the guy who shot up the day care center in Los Angeles. It's certainly there, but that's not where it comes from. It comes from the corporate boardrooms and the individual bedrooms throughout this society.

Truth must speak to power. It's why we must speak out against the exploitation of women like Bathsheba. She is not even named in the scripture we read today. She's called "the wife of Uriah," not even named. In the genealogy of Jesus in Matthew's Gospel, there are five women who are mentioned. Four of them are named, but the fifth, Bathsheba, is not named. There, too, she is called "the wife of Uriah." Bathsheba, seen as the property of men! In Nathan's story, which engages and convicts David, she is compared to an animal. We must speak out against the exploitation of women and against the theory of male supremacy, which relegates women to being the property of men. We must stand also against the homophobia and heterosexism that leads to the persecution of gay and lesbian people. These are the folks that Christians love to hate, the folks that we get so riled up about, like David got so upset about the rich man in Nathan's story. Then, scripture reminds us that we "are the man," and we must confess and speak up.

Truth must speak to power. It is our calling, our duty, as the people of God. We may be scared, as Nathan undoubtedly was, as he came to face David. Nathan was scared. He did not burst into David's presence with his prophetic voice. He had to draw a circle and gradually pull David in. We may choose a less direct method of confrontation, as Nathan did, but we must speak truth to power.

Of course, I am assuming that we have a glimpse of the truth that we can speak. I am bold to claim that we at Oakhurst do have a glimpse — not the whole truth, by any means. We have many lessons yet to learn here at Oakhurst. We will continue to need prophets to speak to us here at Oakhurst, but we have learned some truth here. We've learned some truth that must be spoken to power. We've learned some truth here, not because we are good and righteous, but because we've shared our stories, and we have found out that the people we feared, those monsters we thought would destroy us because of different skin colors, different genders, different sexual orientations, different economic categories — they really are our sisters and brothers, the folk for whom our hearts long. That's one of the gifts that Oakhurst has given to me and to many of us — to learn that the monsters that I feared *out there* were really *in here*, inside me; that out there are sisters and brothers to whom I need to listen. We've heard about one another's pain here, and we've helped one another.

We've also seen firsthand here the destructive consequences of power unchecked, of power that doesn't hear prophets. We've seen husbands and fathers cut down by guns. We've heard about our sons and grandsons who get locked up because they're black. We've seen women in our midst who've been abused by men. We've held hands with people who are poor, who are exploited by society, and then tossed away. We know these stories. We've heard them. We've lived them. We are these stories.

We know firsthand the need to speak truth to power. Oh yes, we continue to need prophetic voices in our midst to speak to us here at Oakhurst. But we also need the courage to be prophetic voices in our community, as Nathan was to David. Truth must speak to power. That was Nathan's calling. It was Nathan's gift to David and to Israel and to us. David didn't hear Nathan's prophecy as a gift, but it was his gift to David. It is one of the reasons that Israel remembers David with such affection, because David was deepened by Nathan's prophecy. We continue to need to listen to one another, to hear Nathan's voice in our midst. We continue to need to seek discernment for those places where we must

listen for that prophetic voice and where we must be that prophetic voice. May God give us the humility to listen for those
voices. May God give us the courage to be those voices. The events
of this week and this year cry out to us. Truth must speak to power.
It is our duty, it is our calling, and it is our survival. Amen.

Editor's Afterword

Nibs Stroupe's challenging and invigorating vision of the radically inclusive identity of the church, and of the prophetic message and mission funded by this identity, sounds clearly from every page of this collection of sermons. This vision is indeed a pearl of great price for the American church in this time and place. In the few pages that follow I want to reflect upon two essential, if somewhat less explicit, dimensions of this vision that are at work in Stroupe's preaching. In my introduction to these sermons I stressed that Stroupe's vision of both church identity and mission are unapologetically grounded in an understanding of the One who calls (and sustains) church and world into being and into relationship: the God witnessed to in the biblical story and known in the history, person, and work of Jesus Christ. Now I would like to look more closely at these grounds, the fundamental hermeneutical and theological assumptions and commitments out of which this vision (and the sermons that proclaim it) grows and by which it is nurtured.

A Biblical Hermeneutics Of Story, Interstice, And Difference

Stroupe's strong sense of story is perhaps the most pivotal dimension of his hermeneutical approach to the biblical text. What kind of God emerges from such a reading? What kind of God is then proclaimed in the act of preaching? For Stroupe, we know God as God is portrayed in the biblical story, as a character and agent in the story: deciding, acting, feeling, loving, hating, judging, and saving. This is a God in passionate and personal relation to the world and to humanity. This God is to be found, and known, in time, in history, indeed, in the midst of our own stories and the stories of others.

For Stroupe, the human predicament is also best understood in terms of story. We have a past, we are journeying through the present, and heading into a future. We are stuck, caught, stretched out, in time. Our finitude and mortality are inherently temporal in nature, and it is precisely in this predicament and on this journey

151

that the God of the Bible engages not only the human characters in the biblical story, but engages us as contemporary readers and interpreters of that story. Stroupe understands one of the tasks for preaching, then, as engineering an encounter between God's story — or, perhaps more accurately, between the God who emerges within the biblical story — and our own story. Stroupe consistently endeavors to create a space in which the biblical story can be heard and appropriated as our own, a space in which we can find, in the biblical story, the truth of our own story.

But this is tricky ground. For Stroupe, the appropriation of the biblical story as our own is not a simple and obvious matter. That the biblical story is indeed our own story, that it speaks a fundamental truth about our lives, is not in any way self-evident. Indeed, such a claim cuts *against* the grain of our common sense self-understanding, especially as that self-understanding is determined by our historical and cultural context. In this respect, the biblical story is *not* our own story. It has, for Stroupe, an independence, and indeed, a certain authority over against our historically and culturally determined values, which come complete with their own interpretive lenses, and by which we seek to discover God and ourselves in scripture, and thereby justify those very values and the sense of meaning and justification they give to our lives. For Stroupe, the meaning of the biblical story is *not* to be confused with an expression of our highest and best aspirations and possibilities as they are currently understood within our contemporary cultural milieu. This would be to appropriate the biblical story into our own story, rather than *vice versa*.

Stroupe never allows the biblical text to simply mirror our best (or worst) modern, liberal instincts or our best (or worst) traditional, conservative commitments. The God who emerges from, and calls to us from the biblical story is most often a strange and unwelcome God to liberal and conservative, both. Regardless of whether we are liberal or conservative (either politically or theologically), this is not the God we bargained for. Stroupe witnesses to this irreducible freedom and strangeness of the God of the Bible with his recurrent refrain that the biblical story — or, the Word addressed to us in the biblical story — is always Bad News as well as Good News. And, consequently, to appropriate the biblical story as the truth of our own story is always in some measure to experience a kind of death, the death of our identity as it is grounded in anything other than our reality as children of the God who addresses us in the Bible. To appropriate the biblical story as our own story is always a passage of mourning and grieving, a passage across a boundary, from death to life. Stroupe preaches from this interstice between the biblical story and our own story. His preaching always witnesses to the irreducible difference between the biblical story and our story, even as it calls us to cross that boundary, to traverse that distance, to die that death and make that passage from death to life and appropriate the biblical story as our own truth; an appropriation in which our story is taken up into the story of the Bible, rather than *vice versa*.

The trickiness of Stroupe's hermeneutical ground is not, however, thereby made firm and free of risk. Stroupe is also careful to witness to the difference between the biblical story and what could be called *God's* own story. This is necessary inasmuch as Stroupe understands the biblical text to reflect the brokenness and sinfulness of its human authors. For Stroupe, the Bible reflects the ways in which its human authors are themselves enslaved to the idols of the world as they emerge and hold sway within the authors' own historical and cultural contexts. Consequently, biblical texts are often silent with regard to certain realities of injustice and oppression — slavery and patriarchy, for example — that define, and hold sway within, the cultural and historical contexts in which they were written. Stroupe is aware of how an unreflective and uncritical identification of the biblical story can entail 1) an uncritical affirmation of the continuing forms of those structures of injustice and oppression in our own time, and 2) an internalization of those structures as integral to our identity. This is the biblical story functioning as bad news in a sense that is divorced from and in opposition to the Good News. This is the bad news of the destructiveness of sin and injustice, of slavery to the idols of the world, and the triumph of the power of death. This is *not* the Bad News mentioned previously as descriptive of our negative experience of the strangeness and freedom of the God of the Bible in relation to our historically and culturally determined identities, values, and desires.[1] This is *not* the Bad News of the biblical story as it resists and judges our desire to have God on our own terms. This is *not* the Bad News that is entailed in the journey of faith as a passage from death to life. This is the Bad News of death triumphant.

This ever-present toxic possibility of the biblical text requires a reading of *resistance*. Stroupe reminds us that we must always recognize and signal the ways in which the structures of injustice and oppression are reflected in the biblical story itself, and that they must be resisted rather than appropriated. This toxic dimension of the biblical story is *not* to be identified with God's movement toward us and with us amidst our journey and within our story. It is *not* to be appropriated as the truth of our identity revealed in God's call and address to us. We are to resist the temptation to simply collapse the biblical story and God's story into a simple, unqualified identity.

Stroupe, then, engages in a kind of double reading of the biblical text. Even as he creates a space in which the biblical story can be heard and appropriated as our own — a space in which we can find, in the biblical story, Good News — he also reads it resistively, highlighting those levels at which the text itself reflects the bad news of the reality of injustice, oppression, and the power of death. This double reading is the result of the extent to which Stroupe reads the biblical text from the interstice of irreducible difference between God's story, the biblical story, our own story — and *the stories of others*. Stroupe's readings of the Bible (and references to theological tradition) are always in response to the diversity of stories that constitute the life of the Oakhurst congregation. These are, inescapably, stories of difference, the difference of race, class, gender, or sexual orientation. For Stroupe, the church is, and must be, continually converted through these encounters with difference through the discovery of others as genuine subjects of their own life with God and as reading subjects with their own experience of the Bible, in other words, as brothers and sisters in Christ. Indeed, this story of continual conversion is Oakhurst's, and Stroupe's, own story.

We have listened to one another's stories here [at Oakhurst], and we have discovered that the people we feared, those monsters we thought would destroy us — because of different skin colors, different genders, different sexual orientations, different economic categories — they are really our sisters and brothers, the folks for whom our hearts long. (see "Truth Speaks To Power," on p. 148 of this book)

Theological Grounds: Freedom Of The Word, Tragic Slavery To The Idols, And Alternative Reality In Christ

Theologically, Stroupe brings together strong traditions of diverse, even conflictual perspectives with a passionate dexterity not easily believed:

- the Reformed tradition's sense for the freedom of God's Word from our own historically and culturally determined assumptions and categories;
- Karl Barth's commitment to God's revelation in Jesus Christ as the central source of our knowledge of God;
- Paul Tillich's concern with culture and his tragic-existentialist understanding of the human predicament;
- liberation, feminist, womanist, and gay and lesbian critiques of the church and its theological tradition, grounded in the particularity of their experiences of God, the Bible, and the Christian life from their various positions of marginalization and oppression; and
- a post-liberal sense for narrative.

In the limited space remaining I will highlight several of these theological dimensions of Stroupe's preaching that are particularly central to and evident in this collection.

Stroupe's commitment to the Reformed understanding of the freedom of the Word of God is at work in a unique way in his annual series of sermons during Black History Month. For Stroupe, the Word is free to address us in the stories and voices of history that call to us from outside any strictly determined border marking

155

off the particular history of the church and its theological tradition. Consequently, every year, during the month of February, Stroupe preaches a series of sermons featuring the stories of key figures in African-American history who contributed to the struggle for the freedom, equality, human dignity, and civil rights of black folk. Though many of these figures and their stories coincide with the history of the black church in America, this is not always the case, and even when there is such a coincidence, as in the obvious case of Martin Luther King, Jr., the stories recounted by Stroupe are played out on the public stage of American history. These sermons are not primarily constituted as interpretations of a passage of scripture, though there is some connection drawn with biblical readings for that day. Neither are they reflections upon the theological work of a key figure within the tradition of the church as it is classically conceived. However, Stroupe presents these figures as members of that "great cloud of witnesses" who have gone before us, bearing witness — in their lives of courage and sacrifice in the fight for justice — to the Good News the church knows, and is called to proclaim, in Jesus Christ: we are all children of God, belonging to God and to one another. These figures are included in that great cloud of witnesses from whom the church has received its faith, hope, and mission, and before whom the church is held accountable for its own continuing witness to the Good News known in Jesus Christ, a witness which must always entail a taking up of the fight for justice, and an imitation of the courage and sacrifice of those who have gone before us in that fight.

There is a dimension of complexity to Stroupe's preaching in this regard that is central to the particular context of Oakhurst Presbyterian Church. I have suggested that, for Stroupe, the stories and the voices of black history in America are vehicles through which the Word, in its freedom, addresses the church from beyond the strict borders of its own scriptural and theological traditions. This is true for the entire Oakhurst congregation in its unity as a community that is both historically determined by these traditions and addressed by the Word in its freedom. But there is a complication to be considered with regard to Oakhurst. The stories and voices of black history also function as stories and voices from the outside in relation to the particular population of *white America*, and this is true for the white folk who make up roughly half of the congregation at Oakhurst. They hear these stories and voices as the Word of God addressing them — addressing and judging in freedom — from the outside. However, for the African-Americans who make up the other half of the congregation hearing Stroupe preach, the stories and voices of black history are *our* stories and *our* voices. They are stories and voices witnessing to how God enters, meets us, and journeys with us through *our* history. This difference is unavoidable at Oakhurst, and is often conflictual. But it is celebrated nonetheless. In the light of Oakhurst's self-understanding as a community of hearers of the Word, it just might become possible, within the context of that community, to begin to hear through the ears of those who are different, without denying that difference and unjustly co-opting their stories as one's own. It just might become possible, as brothers and sisters in Christ, to hear the Word of God that is always free from our own stories and voices, and therefore always entailing a word of judgment, yet nevertheless, as an expression of that very freedom, is a Word that freely and decisively enters our stories to journey with us in our history, to claim us, and bind us to one another, as daughters and sons.

Stroupe's fundamental theological assumption of the freedom of the Word of God to address us ever anew both from within and without the traditional theological and institutional categories of the church and church proclamation is organically linked to his equally nuanced understanding of sin. As tragically vulnerable and broken, as well as ineradicably and stubbornly sinful human beings, we are forever, to borrow a phrase from Karl Barth, turning the Word of God into the word of man. (I intentionally use Barth's gendered pronoun for humanity, here, inasmuch as it signifies, beyond Barth's original intention, the extent to which the word spoken by the church has entailed, and continues to entail, the suppression and exclusion of the voices of women.) For Stroupe, we are forever attempting to lay claim to the Word, to seize it, to domesticate and possess it, in an insatiable desire to have God and the world on our own terms. We want to re-assure ourselves of

157

control and security in the face of chaos and mortality, to separate and insulate ourselves from those who are different and in whom we locate the threat to ourselves, to God's gracious plan for our lives and for creation. The church's turning of the Word of God into the word of man always results in the damage, oppression, and exclusion of others.

Stroupe's bracing and thoroughgoing portrayal of the sinfulness of humanity and its destructive consequences for self, neighbor, and creation, while clearly signaling the extent to which he stands firmly within the Reformed tradition, is nevertheless tempered in several interesting ways by a theological anthropology that appears, at some moments, to have more in common with Schleiermacher and Tillich than with Calvin and Barth. First of all, even in our fallen state, human beings are not simply created beings in rebellion against their creator, but created beings who are fundamentally defined and determined by a deep and ineradicable yearning and longing for God as our source, our center, our home. Nevertheless, we reject God *as God chooses to come to us in freedom* — in the alien strangeness of scripture, in the offensive intimacy of the incarnation and the cross, in the audacious unbelievability of the resurrection, in the threatening proximity of the face, hands, and voice of the neighbor and stranger. Instead, we deal with our fundamental yearning for God by placing our faith and our security in, and by grounding our identities in, the idols and definitions of the world.

For Stroupe, then, human sinfulness is not simply defined as, or rooted in, a primordial and inherent rebellion against God that determines our status before God in a thoroughgoing and absolute way as deserving of absolute and irrevocable divine wrath, judgment, and rejection. Stroupe nuances his understanding of sin with a certain tragic understanding of the existential predicament of the human condition. Our turning away from God as the center of our lives to find our security and identity in the idols of the world is not merely an unmitigated act of prideful rebellion, but rather an act of desperation and fear. To be a fallen human being is to experience, either consciously or unconsciously, our finitude and mortality as alienation and threat. The true source of this experience of finitude and mortality as alienation and threat is our separation from God as the center of our lives and our true definition. This experience is, in fact, an expression of our fundamental yearning for God as creator, center, and home. However, we turn to the idols of the world — rather than to God — to meet and answer this longing because the idols of the world appear to us as more immediate, certain, and reliable sources of security and control. According to Stroupe, we ultimately turn to the idols of the world out of our brokenness and desperation for re-assurance, and not merely out of our prideful rebellious lust for power in opposition to God's sovereignty as Creator and Lord.

Why is it that the idols of the world appear as more immediate and compelling answers to the existential predicament of human life than the true answer itself? For Stroupe, the theological answer is the doctrine of original sin, but again, a doctrine of original sin that is mitigated by a tragic sensibility. The idols of the world appear as immediate and compelling, and indeed, irresistible answers to the anxiety, uncertainty, and desperation of human existence because they are already woven into our identities and relation to the world as we mature from infancy into an independent and responsible individual. We are taught the worship of the idols of the world by the parents, families, communities, traditions, and cultures that give us life, and nurture us into individuality and personhood. The result is that the idols of the world are so inextricably intertwined with our identities, even as children, that we are truly enslaved to them. Stroupe affirms the biblical witness and the theological tradition, then, in their description of the fallen human condition as one of slavery to sin. It is with regards to the process of enslavement that certain echoes of modern liberal and existentialist theological voices can be heard in Stroupe's preaching. We inherit original sin, not through birth so much as through maturation; not through nature so much as through nurture.

Should Stroupe, then, be understood as ultimately soft on sin? I think not. First of all, the devastating destructiveness of sin, of our turning to the idols of the world, is a bold thread running through each and every sermon. Indeed, it is at the heart of the litany that is repeated in some form each Sunday at Oakhurst, either in sermon, pastoral prayer, or liturgy: our worship of racism, sexism, homophobia, class, consumerism, and militarism is radically destructive of human beings and creation. Secondly, as suggested above, the sense of enslavement to sin central to traditional formulations of the doctrine of original sin does indeed find unflinching, rigorous, and thoroughgoing expression in Stroupe's more nuanced treatment. What is more, I believe this to be one of if not the most critical and invaluable theological insights funding Stroupe's theological and pastoral vision. As I began to say above, for Stroupe, we are taught the worship of the idols of the world — racism, sexism, homophobia, consumerism, and militarism; all the powers of death — not only by secular, blaspheming, godless sinners, but by pious, Christian, God-fearing folk, by those very people who gave us life and who nurtured us and who loved us. Similarly, we are taught to worship the powers of death by those very traditions that taught us both the value of life and life-giving values, such as freedom, self-respect, equality, and dignity. What is more, for those raised in the church, the parents, the families, the communities, and the traditions that gave us the gift of faith, that taught us about the love of God and shaped our identities by the stories of God's movement in history and the Good News of the gospel, also taught us to worship the idols of the world and shaped our identities by an unquestioning faith in the power of death. This, again, not because they are especially wicked people, but because they themselves were raised, taught, and shaped under the same tragically complex conditions. They do this not out of their wickedness, but out of their own tragically determined uncertainty and desperation, out of their own enslavement to the idols of the world.

The key point for Stroupe here is not to trace this cycle back to a primordial fall in the garden. Rather, the important point is the extent to which it is impossible to separate and isolate goodness and righteousness from sin and evil. It is impossible to locate and isolate sin and evil in a particular location outside ourselves, to identify sin and evil with a particular people, community, or culture different than our own. There is no ground of purity, no possibility of purity. We inherit sin from those same folk from whom we inherit our Christian faith. The sources and resources of justice, righteousness, and goodness are always complicit in some fundamental way with the sources and resources of injustice, sin, and evil. In the tragic context of our finite, created reality, they are never absolutely separable. This is the predicament in which we live, and this is the predicament into which God enters and meets us and journeys with us. Perhaps more importantly, this is the predicament, then, to which God is subjected and made vulnerable. God chooses to enter into vulnerability to, and thereby risk complicity with, the forces of sin and evil.

Stroupe often speaks of God's surprising, and indeed, seemingly inappropriate, if not offensive, decision to entrust the proclamation of the gospel to broken, troubled, and sinful human beings, human beings who inevitably turn the redeeming Word of God into the destructive word of man. God entrusts the gospel to the disciples, who, as portrayed in the gospels, are clearly inadequate to the task, and through them to the early church, which, as portrayed in Paul's letters, manages from the very beginning to repeatedly bungle the job. The early church established a track record from which the church has not deviated for two millennia, leaving in its wake a history of irrecuperable damages from an unending series of complicities with the powers, principalities, and idols of the world. Because of God's choice to meet us, encounter us, call us into relationship, and journey with us in covenant partnership within our own fragile, broken, and sinful history, the church's proclamation of the Good News of the gospel is never proclaimed and/or encountered free of such complicities. Consequently, in one of Stroupe's more recurrent phrases, the church is always "*bold* to claim," for example, to claim that Jesus Christ is Lord. The church is "bold to claim" because such a claim is always a risky business. It is always complicit with and compromised by the historical failures of those making the claim. In the realm of public history and public discourse, there is always a sense of the unwarranted, and the presumptuous, and even the irresponsible and the dangerous in church proclamation.

For Stroupe, the church is not afforded the privilege or even the possibility of separating itself out from the world into a realm purified by its own proclamation and seeming "possession" of the

161

Good News of Jesus Christ, a realm of purity in which its hands are not bloodied with multiple complicities. For it was and is God's good pleasure — surprising and wonderful, strange and troubling — to give up that privilege and possibility, and it is precisely this God that the church knows in the history of Israel and in Jesus Christ, and to whom it is called to witness. I would argue, then, that while seemingly qualified and softened by a liberal sensibility and anthropology, Stroupe's treatment of sin nevertheless entails radical theological claims about 1) the ubiquity, inescapability, and destructiveness of sin, 2) the self-critical limits of the church's own relation to, understanding of, and proclamation of the gospel, and 3) perhaps most radical of all, about who *God* is, and what God risks in being irrevocably *for and with us.*

For Stroupe, then, humanity's fallen condition, both sinful and tragic, consists in our enslavement to the idols of the world. We turn to the definitions and categories of the world — racism, sexism, consumerism, classism, homophobia, and militarism — for meaning, certainty, and security. We turn to these definitions and categories to ground our own identities and our understanding of and relation to reality. It is these definitions and categories that separate us from the neighbor, convincing us that those for whom our heart longs are a threat, are enemies to be feared, excluded, eliminated. This is the power of death that governs our lives, both individual and communal. The definitions and categories of the world are allowed to determine and define reality to such an extent that we are unable to imagine any alternative possibilities. The reality of the world is under the rule of the power of death, a closed system without true possibility, a closed system, for example, where possibility can only be conceived in terms of the inevitable play of "the market" and "economic forces."

Stroupe is convinced that it is in, and to, this world that the church is called to boldly proclaim another reality, the reality known in Jesus Christ. This other reality is our true reality as children of God who belong to God and to one another. In a world governed by the power of death, this alternative reality is constituted by openness and possibility. In a world governed by the power of death, this alternative reality of possibility, though it is our true reality, is truly *alternative*. It does not show up on the radar of reality defined by the categories of the world and governed by the power of death. Stroupe is clear that in a world governed by the power of death, this reality of openness and possibility, though it is our true reality, can only appear as an *impossibility*. It cannot be demonstrated by, in, and with the available and culturally validated terms and assumptions. It can only be witnessed to by a bold, strange, audacious, and in some contexts, offensive proclamation and testimony. This proclamation and testimony is always vulnerable to contestation and dismissal as constituting an *un*realistic, fanciful and irresponsible *flight from* true reality. Indeed, for Stroupe, it cannot *appear* at all to an understanding of reality governed by the power of death. It can only be envisioned by a passionate imagination fired by bold and unlikely witness, proclamation and testimony, fired by the unlikely and surprising event of being addressed by the free and gracious Word of God, fired by the unlikely and surprising — indeed, impossible — event of hearing your name called by the risen Jesus in the very midst of a world governed by the power of death.

This, of course, is the story of Mary's encounter with the risen Jesus in the graveyard. It is therefore no surprise that Stroupe's sermon on this biblical story, "Walking Through The Graveyard," is both the frontispiece and — along with the final sermon of this collection, "Truth Speaks To Power" — the centerpiece of this collection. The latter sermon is central to Stroupe's theological vision in that it brings into focus the necessities and risks not only of witnessing to and *proclaiming* the alternative reality seen, heard, and known in Jesus Christ, but of responding to and living in accordance with that reality. Just as the proclamation of the church cannot escape the risk of bold audacity. Just so, individual and communal life in accordance with that proclamation will always be moving against the stream of prevailing social and political culture to the extent that they uncritically assume the authority of and are funded by the definitions and categories of the world. For Stroupe, the church's bold proclamation that Jesus Christ is Lord must necessarily be fleshed out in, and is meaningless, unwarranted, and dangerous in the absence of, a life of resistance to the

163

idols of the world. Such proclamation must be fleshed out in resistance to the powers and principalities as they are incarnated within the governmental, economic, juridical, and cultural structures, systems and institutions of nations, societies, and communities, both large and small, both local and global.

A Final Plug:
Displacing The Conservative-Liberal Opposition

Because of the unique complexity of his commitment to the biblical story and theological tradition's witness to Jesus Christ on the one hand, and the diverse stories and experiences of the Oakhurst congregation's journey and work on the other, Stroupe's sermons constitute a unique and much needed displacement of the polarized liberal-conservative divide within the American church. It is eminently clear that Stroupe's liberal vision of radically inclusive and egalitarian church membership is not simply the result of a dismissal of either the authority of the biblical text or the particularity of Jesus Christ — the two pillars upon which conservatives consistently justify their own dismissal of such a vision as illegitimate for Christian faith and practice. Likewise, it is precisely Stroupe's uncompromising biblical and theological commitments which make it impossible to reduce the gospel proclaimed in his preaching to a liberal-humanist vision wholly continuous with the day's highest and most progressive ethical and cultural instincts and sensitivities. The liberal temptation to such a reduction is typically governed by the assumption that all "orthodox" (biblical, doctrinal, creedal) theological claims — claims regarding the God known in Jesus Christ as the center of our lives, of the life of the church, and of creation; a God by whose uncompromising claim of love we are defined, and to which we are accountable — constitute a distraction from, if not obstacle to, the work of justice in the community, the nation, and the world. Consequently, Stroupe offers a displacement of the polarized opposition of liberals and conservatives within the American church that cuts both ways, resisting the hardened assumptions of both parties, and thereby opening the rare possibility of engagement in place of blind polemics.

1. The capital letters of "Bad News," here, are meant to signify the judgment of God upon our attempts to ground our identity and have the world on terms other than God's grace — a judgment that is theologically determined by, limited by and circumscribed within the Good News of that very graciousness: this Bad News is not *really* bad for us and for creation, not truly harmful or destructive; we only *experience* it that way in our resistance to the true source of our life and well-being — God's grace. This grammatical mark signifying this very specific theological determination is meant to distinguish this sense of Bad News from the sense of bad news determined as historical violence and damage to our (and others') identities and to the world as God's good creation, as recipients of God's grace — a bad news that *is* really bad for us, that is *not* specifically entailed within and determined by the Good News, but is the fruit of our opposition to the Good News.

Pres.   no bishops
      distrust centralized power

see foreword

power sharing   is hardest for whites
    pro Gay
rejects dichotomy of political / theological